ALGEBRA PUZZLERS

by Theresa Kane McKell

Teacher Reviewer
Nan Wilson

Senior Editor
Kristin Eclov

Editor
Karen P. Hall

Production and Design
Amy Dohmen

Illustrator
Tani Brooks Johnson

Cover Design
Anthony D. Paular

McGraw-Hill
Children's Publishing

A Division of The McGraw-Hill Companies

Published by Good Apple
An imprint of McGraw-Hill Children's Publishing
Copyright © 1998 McGraw-Hill Children's Publishing

Send all inquiries to:
McGraw-Hill Children's Publishing
3195 Wilson Drive NW
Grand Rapids, Michigan 49544

Algebra Puzzlers
ISBN: 0-7682-0101-2

TABLE OF CONTENTS

TABLE OF CONTENTS

TABLE OF CONTENTS

Solving Square Roots and Quadratic Equations

Simplifying Polynomials

Answer Key

ABOUT THIS BOOK

Your students will look forward to math with fun-filled *Algebra Puzzlers*. More than just worksheets, these practice pages offer a wide variety of enticing, challenging math puzzles that include fascinating facts about the world in which we live. Also included on each page is a helpful tip to remind students of important algebraic facts, figures, and formulas. All major algebra concepts are covered—from working with real numbers and linear equations to simplifying exponents and polynomials. Watch your students eagerly practice their math skills as they solve "puzzling" problems and discover answers to trivia teasers.

GETTING STARTED

- The puzzles are organized by subject area (e.g., writing linear equations). Refer to the table of contents or look at the bottom of the puzzler pages to see which subject area is being reinforced.

- Each puzzle focuses on a specific math skill (e.g., writing equations in slope-intercept form), which is listed (in parenthesis) in the table of contents and in the upper right-hand corner of every puzzler page.

- Select puzzles that best meet your students' needs. Always review relevant math concepts before having students work independently.

- Give each student a copy of the Algebra Tip Sheet (page 7). As students complete the puzzler pages, have them record on the tip sheet important facts they learn about algebra concepts. Encourage students to refer to their tip sheets as they complete the Review What You Know page at the end of each section.

- Invite students to self-check their work. Write the answers to the math problems (see Answer Key, pages 103–112) on the chalkboard or on separate index cards stored in a recipe box. Have students redo problems they miss and note ways in which they can improve their skills.

- Use the Review What You Know pages along with the Algebra Checklist (page 6) to assess students' understanding of specific algebra concepts. Have one-on-one conferences with students to discuss their progress.

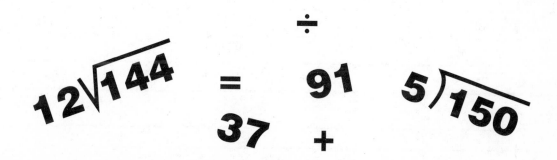

ALGEBRA CHECKLIST

Student: _____   Class Period: _____

SKILL	MASTERY LEVEL		
	Experiencing Difficulty	Working Toward Mastery	Complet Mastery
Adding and subtracting real numbers			
Multiplying and dividing real numbers			
Solving for x and y in linear equations			
Using x- and y-intercepts to draw linear graphs			
Using slopes and coordinate pairs to draw linear graphs			
Drawing graphs of equations in slope-intercept form			
Writing equations in standard form			
Writing equations in slope-intercept form			
Writing equations in point-slope form			
Solving absolute-value equations			
Drawing graphs of absolute-value equations			
Solving inequality equations			
Drawing graphs of inequality equations			
Solving linear systems			
Drawing graphs of linear systems			
Simplifying exponents			
Writing in scientific notation			
Solving equations that involve square roots			
Using the Pythagorean formula			
Using the quadratic formula			
Drawing graphs of quadratic equations			
Adding and subtracting polynomials			
Multiplying polynomials			
Factoring polynomials			

COMMENTS _____

_____

_____

_____

_____

ALGEBRA TIP SHEET

TOPIC		TIP
Order of Operations	💡	Solve what's in parenthesis first.

Name: _____ Date: _____ Class: _____

Graphs for _____
(title of worksheet)

Name: _____   Date: _____   Class: _____

RIVER RAPIDS

The Nile River is the longest river in the world, measuring 4,160 miles. In which continent is it located?

Solve each problem. Shade in the grid boxes that contain your solutions. Read across the remaining unshaded boxes to spell out the answer to the question.

 Tip: Follow the **order of operations** when solving problems that involve a series of calculations. The order to complete the calculations are powers (exponents) first, then multiplication and division, and then addition and subtraction.
For example, $34 - 3^2 \times 2 \rightarrow 34 - 9 \times 2 \rightarrow 34 - 18 \rightarrow 16$.

1. $4 + 6 - 10 \div 2$

2. $45 \div 3 \times 20 + 4^2$

3. $6 \times 5 - 7 \times 3$

4. $16 - 6 + 2 \div 2$

5. $50 \times 2 \div 10^2$

6. $34 \div 17 + 4$

7. $8^2 \div 16 \times 2$

8. $17 \times 2 - 102 \div 3$

9. $6 - 2 + 10 \times 2^2$

10. $4^3 - 4 - 8 \times 7$

11. $10 \times 3 + 1 - 16$

12. $13 + 8^2 - 24$

13. $54 \div 27 \times 3 + 6$

14. $19 - 2^2 \times 4$

15. $9 + 5 - 16 \div 4$

16. $3 \times 6 + 2 + 5$

17. $9 \times 3 \div 3 + 4^2 - 1$

18. $6 \times 2 + 14 \div 7$

H 15	P 12	I 0	A 29	J 316	F 67	G 1	Y 8
R 66	C 25	D 53	F 9	K 11	I 2	U 3	Q 4
X 44	L 24	G 6	C 55	Z 10	A 101	P 14	I 5

Answer: _____

Name: _____   Date: _____   Class: _____

GOOD OWL TIME

Where do owls stay when they take a trip?

Solve each equation. To spell out the answer to the riddle, write the letter of the corresponding problem above the given answer.

 Tip: When using the **order of operations**, solve what's in parenthesis first. For example,
$(13 + 7) - 2^2 \times 3 \rightarrow 20 - 2^2 \times 3 \rightarrow 20 - 4 \times 3 \rightarrow 20 - 12 = 8$.

A. $24 - 12 \div 2$

B. $(3 \times 20) - 3^2 + 45$

C. $25 - (11 \times 2) + 6$

D. $14 - 6 \div 2 + 5$

E. $64 \div (9 \times 3 - 19)$

F. $18 + 3 - 12 \div 6$

G. $6^2 \div 9 \times 5$

H. $40 \times 3 + 12 - 1$

I. $4 + 10 \times 2^3 - 16$

J. $100 - [108 \div (9 - 5)]$

K. $51 \div 17 + 4 \times 3$

L. $11 \times 11 + 121 \div 11 - 11$

M. $3^3 \div 3 + 169 \div 13$

N. $4^2 \times 5 \times 6 \div 3 + 10$

O. $100 \div 5^2 + 10$

P. $42 \div 3 + (6^2 - 8)$

R. $21 + 10^2 \div 10$

S. $6 \times 5 + 32 \div 4$

T. $8 - 6 + 27 \div 3^2$

U. $7^2 + 10 - 2 \times 5$

Answer:

___ ___ ___ ___ ___ ___ ___ ___ ___
18   5   18   131   14   14   5   8   121

me: Date: Class:

EXCUSES

What is one of the worst excuses for not turning in your homework?

Solve each problem. Write the exercise number in front of the corresponding answer listed in the grid. To spell out the answer at the bottom of the page, refer to the grid and write the code letter that corresponds to the exercise number given.

 Tip: Use the **properties for addition** when adding real numbers. The equations to remember are $a + 0 = a$ and $a + (-a) = 0$; and $a + b = b + a$ and $-(a + b) = -a + (-b)$. For example, $-(4 + 9) + 2 + (-2) \rightarrow -4 + (-9) + 2 + (-2) \rightarrow -13$.

1. $-(8 + 20)$	11. $10 + (-16) + 4$
2. $5 + (-11) + 2$	12. $-14 + 13 + (-4)$
3. $13 + (-4) + (-5)$	13. $-5 + (-3) + 8$
4. $-2 + (-11) + (-7)$	14. $-[(-2) + (-6)]$
5. $0 + (-10)$	15. $-5 + (-6) + (-20)$
6. $-4 + (-12) + (-3)$	16. $15.3 + (-12.4)$
7. $-[13 + (-7)]$	17. $-13.8 + (-16.4)$
8. $2 + (-11) + 14$	18. $5.8 + 7.3 + (-12.1)$
9. $42 + 10 + (-50)$	19. $-12 + (-1.1) + (-2.3)$
10. $-22 + 15 + 10$	20. $6.5 + 3.5 + (-6.5)$

Code Letter	Exercise #	Answer
A		−10
B		−6
C		−15.4
D		−4
E		−19
F		3.5
G		−5
H		4
I		5
K		1
L		3
M		−20
N		−31
O		−28
P		−2
R		2
S		8
T		−30.2
U		0
Y		2.9

Answer:

___ ___ ___ ___   ___ ___   ___ ___
8   14   5   17   1   15   4   16

___ ___ ___ ___ ___ ___   ___ ___ ___   ___ ___ ___
11   6   15   19   8   10   5   15   2   12   1   17

___ ___ ___ ___   ___ ___ ___ ___ ___ ___ ___ ___ ___ !
10   6   5   2   11   1   8   14   1   15   8   15   12

Reproducible

Name: Date: Class:

GNARLY NEGATIVES

Kalyan Ramji Sain of Sundargarth, India, made the *Guinness Book of World Records* with this 133 $\frac{1}{2}$-inch facial phenomenon. What won him the record?

Solve each problem. Draw a line from each problem in Column A to its answer in Column B. Write next to each exercise number the letter that represents each answer. Read down the column of written letters to discover the answer to the world-record question.

 Tip: Use the *subtraction rule*, $a - b = a + (-b)$, when subtracting real numbers. Remember that subtracting a negative is the same as adding a positive.
For example, $-25 - 20 - (-100) \rightarrow -25 + (-20) + 100 \rightarrow -45 + 100 \rightarrow 55$.

Column A

_____ 1. $-3 - (-8)$

_____ 2. $3 - (-6) - 2$

_____ 3. $7 - 12$

_____ 4. $52 - 63$

_____ 5. $5 - 30 - 6 - 35$

_____ 6. $22 - 40$

_____ 7. $-100 - (-10) - 40$

_____ 8. $-12 - 3$

_____ 9. $-90 - (-30)$

_____10. $30 - 32$

_____11. $-17.3 - 2.7 - 3$

_____12. $-11 - (-7)$

_____13. $-12.68 - (-12.68) - 5.3$

_____14. $-2 - 6$

_____15. $0 - 4 + 10 - 6$

Column B

(O) 7

(L) 5

(U) −60

(S) −18

(E) 0

(T) −23

(C) −5.3

(G) −11

(M) −15

(H) −8

(E) −66

(T) −130

(S) −2

(N) −5

(A) −4

Answer: _____

RAPID RABBITS

Why don't rabbits carry calculators?

Solve each problem. To spell out the answer to the rabbit riddle, write the letter of the exercise above the answer given.

 Tip: Addition problems involving a positive and a negative number are solved as if they were subtraction problems. For example $5 + (-3) \rightarrow 5 - 3 \rightarrow 2$.

A. $0 + (-4)$

B. $-25 + (-2)$

C. $-8 + 32$

E. $42 - 45$

H. $68 - (-45)$

I. $-75 - 75$

K. $19 + (-54) - 12$

L. $-120 - 30 + 2 + 30$

M. $-18.3 + 12.5 - (-18.3)$

O. $-3 + 4 + (-2) + 21 + (-12)$

P. $-10 + 9 + (-30) + 30 + 10$

Q. $-15 + 30 + (-15) + (-30) + 1$

S. $5 - (-7) - 30 - 12 - (-30)$

T. $75 - 50 - (-100) - 150$

U. $-14 - (-14) - 25 - 50 - 30$

W. $80 - 100 + 35 - (-80)$

Y. $-5.5 + 6.5 - 1 + 5$

Answer:

-27	-3	24	-4	-105	0	-3		-25	113	-3	5

12.5	-105	-118	-25	-150	9	-118	5		0	8

-29	-105	-150	24	-47	-118	5		95	-150	-25	113	8	-105	-25

-25	113	-3	12.5

Name: Date: Class:

SERIES OF MULTIPLICATION

What baseball team has won the World Series a record of 23 times, more than any other team in the world?

Solve the problems. Circle the letters that represent the solutions. To spell out the answer to the question, copy each circled letter onto the line that is labeled with its corresponding exercise number.

 Tip: When solving problems involving multiplication of real numbers, remember that $(a)(-b) = -ab$ and $(-a)(-b) = ab$. For example, $(-5)(-4)(3a) = 60a$.

1. $(-8)(9)(a)$ R. $36a$

2. $(3)(-4a)$ E. $-12a$

3. $(-5)(6a)$ K. $30a$

4. $(10)(-4a)$ Y. $-40a$

5. $(18)(-2a)$ N. $72a$

6. $(-6)(3)(-2)(a)$ E. $-90a$

7. $(7)(-8)(a)$ O. $-36a$

8. $(-2)(-3a)(-4)$ Y. $-24a$

9. $(-5)(-7a)(-1)$ W. $-30a$

10. $(-4a)(9)(-2)$ E. $60a$

11. $(-3a)(-2)(5)$ N. $-72a$

12. $(-20a)(-3)$ A. $-35a$

13. $(-6a)(-15)(-1)$ S. $56a$

14. $(-2)(-4a)(7)$ K. $-56a$

Answer:

___   ___   ___   ___   ___   ___   ___   ___   ___   ___   ___   ___   ___   ___
1   2   3   4   5   6   7   8   9   10   11   12   13   14

Date: _____   Class: _____

me: _____

CHUGGIN' THROUGH MULTIPLICATION

On August 26, 1989, a train in South Africa carried a record number of 660 cars. What was the length of the train?

The train below is trying to chug along its tracks, but it needs your help to move forward. Solve each problem to help the train reach the finish line. The letters representing the negative answers will spell out the five-word answer to the train trivia.

Tip: The absolute value of a negative is always positive. For example, $|{-}4|(10) \rightarrow (4)(10) \rightarrow 40$.

START

N. $(-5)(-6)$ F. $(-3)(-4)(-5)$ O. $|(-6)|(-20)$ M. $|(-32)(-2)|$

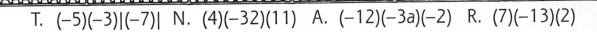

U. $(4)(-1)|(-9)|$

T. $(-5)(-3)|(-7)|$ N. $(4)(-32)(11)$ A. $(-12)(-3a)(-2)$ R. $(7)(-13)(2)$

A. $(5a)(6)(-8)$ H. $(5)(-20)|(-3)|$ O. $(-6)(-4)(3a)$ A. $(-4)(-12)(-7)$

D. $(24)(-2)(-4)(-3)$

L. $(-8)|(-90)|$

I. $(-9)(6)$ U. $(-8)(-9)(0)(-1)$ M. $(-4)(6)(1)$ F. $(2)(-10)|(-8)|$

L. $(-1)(-3)(-1)$

E. $|(2a)|(-100)$ S. $(4)(2)(-12)$ **FINISH**

Answer: _____

th...

Using the Distrubutive Property

Name: _____   Date: _____   Class: _____

NUMBER STUMPER

How well do you know your numbers? Test your knowledge on these challenging number stumpers.

Use the distributive property to determine if the left side of each equation is equal to the right. If both sides are equal, the corresponding statement is true; if both sides are not equal, the statement is false.

 Tip: The distributive property is used to solve multiplication problems involving parenthesis. The equations to remember are $a(b + c) = ab + ac$ and $a(b - c) = ab - ac$ and $-a(b - c) = -ab + ac$. For example, $4(y - 8r) = 4y - 32r$.

1. We use a number system with a base of 10, but any base could be used for a number system.

    $4(y - 6) = 4y - 24$ True or False?

2. Prime numbers are those that can be divided only by themselves and one.

    $(y - 2)(-6) = -6y + 12$ True or False?

3. When a cookie is halved, two people would receive 2 pieces of the cookie each.

    $(11x - 4)(-4) = 44x - 16$ True or False?

4. Numbers less than one can be written as decimals.

    $(13 + 9x)(6) = 78 + 54x$ True or False?

5. The area of any shape is the distance around its surface.

    $(15 - 7x)(-2) = 30 - 14x$ True or False?

Answer: _____

Reproducible

16

© Good Apple GA16

ame: Date: Class:

TREE-MENDOUS MATH

What kind of math do trees learn?

Solve the problems in numerical order, and find the matching solutions in the list provided. Use the corresponding letters to spell out the answer to the tricky tree trivia.

 Tip: Dividing by a number is the same as multiplying by its reciprocal $(a \div b = a \cdot 1/b)$. For example, $-6x = 5 \rightarrow x = 5 \div (-6) \rightarrow x = 5 \cdot (-1/6) \rightarrow x = -5/6$.

1. $18 \div 3$

2. $8 \div 1/2$

3. $-6 \div 6/5$

4. $-5 \div 1/10$

5. $-7x = -21$

6. $-4x = -1$

7. $9 = -36x$

8. $45 = 5x$

9. $-2x = 2$

10. $-30 = -6x$

11. $1/2x = 14$

12. $-x = 13$

G = -50	N = 1/4	T = 5	R = 28
T = 6	E = -1	W = 16	M = 9
O = 3	Y = -13	I = -5	O = -1/4

Answer: _____

th...

Name: Date: Class:

REVIEW WHAT YOU KNOW
ABOUT REAL NUMBERS

Use the order of operations to solve the following problems.

1. 4 x 2 + 7

2. (5 + 4) – 3 x 2

3. [(7 + 6) x 2] + 3

4. (13 – 5 + 6) ÷ 7

5. [10 + 6 ÷ 2] x 3

Add and subtract the following real numbers.

6. –1 – 2 + 3

7. 2 – 5 + 6 – 8

8. 10 – 7 + 6 – 12

9. –2 + 6 – 13 + 20

10. –3 – 7 + 5 – 11

Multiply and divide the following real numbers.
(Remember to use the distributive property when needed.)

11. (–4)(–2)(–6)

12. –3(y + 8)

13. 4/9 ÷ (–4/3)

14. (–2)(–7x – 8)

15. –14 ÷ [2x (– 7)]

Name: Date: Class:

BUILDING NUMBER SENSE

How many feet high is the world's tallest building—the CN Tower in Toronto, Canada?

Simplify each problem. Place each answer in the appropriate position in the crossword puzzle. Read across the rows to identify the highlighted boxes, and write the corresponding numbers in sequence to reveal the answer to the question.

 Tip: When combining like terms, add or subtract the numbers in front of the common variable. For example, $14a + 2a - 15a = 16a - 15a = a$.

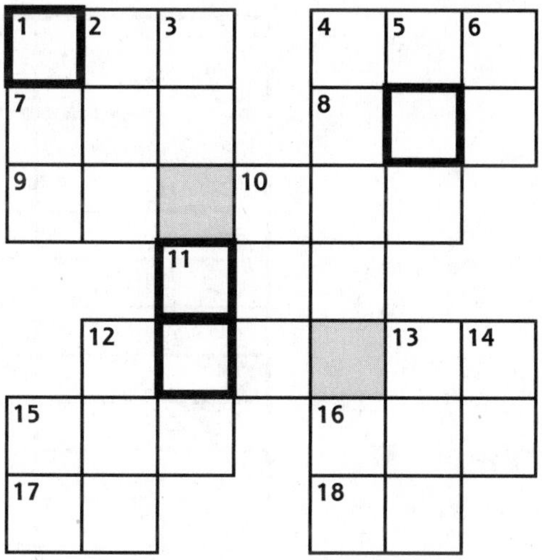

[crossword puzzle grid with numbered cells 1–18]

ACROSS
1. $16x - 2x$
4. $9x + 14x$
7. $26y + 13y$
8. $58y - 10y$
9. $20ax - 19ax$
10. $2ax + 5ax$
11. $5y + 19y$
12. $48x - 20x + 3x$
13. $4x + 10x - 11x$
15. $23x + 25x + 8x$
16. $2xy + 12xy - 9xy$
17. $30xy - 28xy - xy$
18. $22ay + 11ay - 32ay$

DOWN
1. $26a - 14a + a$
2. $75x - 26x$
3. $10xy - 8xy - xy$
4. $12ay + 12ay$
5. $10x + 12x + 16x$
6. $100xy - 90xy - 9xy$
10. $10x + 65x - x$
11. $7x + 19x - 6x + x$
12. $45y - 10y + y$
13. $14xy - 5xy - 6xy$
14. $5xy - 4xy$
15. $80x + 20x - 95x$
16. $25a - 15a - 5a$

Answer: _____

the

Name: Date: Class:

OLD FAITHFUL

Old Faithful is the name of a famous geyser found in which United States national park?

Simplify each problem. Write the exercise number in front of the corresponding answer listed in the grid. To spell out the answer to the trivia question, refer to the grid and write the code letter that corresponds to the exercise number given.

 Tip: When combining like terms, use the distributive property when needed. Remember that unlike terms, those that have different variables, cannot be added together. For example, $-4(3a - 6b) + 5c = -12a + 24b + 5c$.

1. $-8(-x - 3y)$

2. $2(r + s) + r + s$

3. $-2(x + y) + 3(5x - 6y)$

4. $-3(3x + 5y) + 10x + y$

5. $7(2x - 3) + 8x$

6. $-5(a + 7b) + 10(2a + 3b)$

7. $-8(r + 2s) + 5(r + 3s)$

8. $4(-x + 9y) + 7(3x - 7y)$

9. $-6(-2x - 5y) + 6(4x - 5y)$

10. $(3x + 5y) - (2x + 3y)$

11. $-(a + b) + 3(2a + 5b)$

12. $9(x - 3y) + 4(-5x + 2y)$

13. $3(-2a - 5b) - 4(5a + 8b)$

14. $-10(r + s) + 10(r + s)$

15. $-(a - 7b) - (a + 7b)$

Code Letter	Exercise #	Answer
A		$13x - 20y$
C		$x + 2y$
E		$8x + 24y$
H		$3r + 3s$
I		$5a + 14b$
K		$15a - 5b$
L		0
N		$x - 14y$
O		$17x - 13y$
R		$22x - 21$
S		$-11x - 19y$
T		$-2a$
U		$-3r - s$
W		$-26a - 47b$
Y		$36x$

Answer:

____ ____ ____ ____ ____ ____ ____ ____ ____ ____ ____
9   1   14   14   8   13   12   15   8   4   1

Name: Date: Class:

A DEEPER UNDERSTANDING

The deepest ocean is the Pacific Ocean. The ocean bed descends to a record depth of 36,198 feet in the Marianas Trench, located near which group of islands?

Solve the equations in both Column A and Column B. Draw lines to connect the equations that have matching solutions. To spell out the answer to the question, write in front of each exercise number in Column A the letter from the matching equation in Column B.

 Tip: When solving for the variable in an addition problem, you must subtract the same number from both sides of the equation. In a subtraction problem, you must add the same number to both sides. For example, $x + 3 = 4 \rightarrow x + 3 - 3 = 4 - 3 \rightarrow x = 1$.

Column A

_____ 1. $x + 6 = 4$

_____ 2. $5 + x = 50$

_____ 3. $30 = x + 33$

_____ 4. $5 + x = 0$

_____ 5. $7 + x = -1$

_____ 6. $10 + x = 14$

_____ 7. $12 + x = -21$

_____ 8. $9 = x + -2$

_____ 9. $99 + x = 102$

_____10. $x + 14 = 15$

_____11. $25 + x = -5$

Column B

(L) $x - 10 = -15$

(E) $-21 + x = -20$

(P) $2 = x - 2$

(P) $-3 = x - 1$

(S) $x - 5 = -35$

(I) $-30 = x - 27$

(H) $x - 90 = -45$

(N) $-13 = x - 16$

(I) $3 = x - 8$

(P) $-45 = x - 12$

(I) $x - 8 = -16$

ood Apple GA1687

Name: _____   Date: _____   Class: _____

MID-SECTION MEASUREMENT

The Earth's circumference at the equator is 24,847 miles. How many miles is the Earth's diameter at the equator?

Solve for x. Place each answer in the appropriate position in the crossword puzzle. Read across the rows to identify the highlighted boxes, and write the corresponding numbers in sequence to reveal the answer to the question.

 Tip: When solving for the variable in a division problem, you must multiply the same number on both sides of the equation. In a multiplication problem, you must divide the same number on both sides. For example, $x \div 7 = 5 \rightarrow x \div 7 \,(7) = 5\,(7) \rightarrow x = 35$.

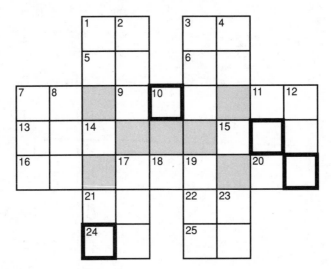

ACROSS
1. $3x = 153$
3. $5x = 55$
5. $168 = 2x$
6. $10x = 450$
7. $4x = 92$
9. $748 = 2x$
11. $6x = 84$
13. $2628 = 3x$
15. $2x = 1392$
16. $10x = 880$
17. $2625 = 3x$
20. $5x = 300$

21. $6x = 384$
22. $378 = 7x$
24. $3x = 273$
25. $400 = 8x$

DOWN
1. $x \div 2 = 29$
2. $x \div 13 = 11$
3. $x \div 12 = 12$
4. $3 = x \div 5$
7. $72 = x \div 4$
8. $x \div 9 = 42$
11. $x \div 2 = 98$
12. $10 = x \div 46$
17. $29 = x \div 29$
19. $x \div 5 = 111$
21. $23 = x \div 3$
23. $x \div 10 = 4$

Answer: _____

Name: _____ Date: _____ Class: _____

SPACE ODYSSEY

The first United States space satellite, Explorer I, and the first manned spacecraft, Apollo II, were launched from the same city in Florida. What is the name of the city?

Solve for x. Shade in the grid boxes that contain your solutions. Read across the remaining unshaded boxes to spell out the answer to the question.

 Tip: When solving a two–step equation that includes a variable preceded by a fraction, isolate the term and then multiply both sides of the equation by the reciprocal. For example, $1/2x + 20 = 30 \rightarrow 1/2x = 10 \rightarrow (2/1)(1/2x) = 10(2/1) \rightarrow x = 20$.

1. $1/3x + 10 = 5$

2. $1/4x + 3 = 10$

3. $1/5x + 2 = 4$

4. $10 + 1/6x = 7$

5. $11 + 1/2x = 24$

6. $1/3x + 7 = 14$

7. $8 + 1/4x = 11$

8. $3 + 1/5x = -10$

9. $1/3x + 23 = 15$

10. $1/2x + 4 = 14$

11. $12 + 1/2x = -24$

12. $2 + 1/3x = -2$

13. $1/4x + 2 = 8$

14. $9 + 1/9x = 9$

15. $1/4x + 5 = 13$

C	W	Y	O	A	L	I
−10	−15	−65	−72	1	28	12
P	M	E	R	S	C	A
5	−24	−19	10	32	−21	72
J	N	T	A	Q	V	E
−12	25	21	−11	−18	−1	15
X	R	B	A	Z	L	S
20	23	0	−62	26	19	24

Answer: _____

Name: _____   Date: _____   Class: _____

SINGLED OUT

His single, "White Christmas," has sold over 30 million copies and currently holds the title Best-Selling Single Worldwide. Who was the famous singer?

Solve each equation for x. Compare the answers of each pair and circle the letter of the one with the greater value. Write the circled letters in the order they appear to spell out the answer to the "musical" question.

 Tip: When solving two-step equations that require multiplying or dividing by a negative number, remember that $(-a)(-b) = ab$ and $-a \div -b = a/b$. For example,
$-5x + 4 = -21 \rightarrow -5x = -25 \rightarrow -5x \div (-5) = -25 \div (-5) \rightarrow x = 5$.

1. (A) $3x - 5 = 16$

    (B) $4x - 10 = 30$

2. (E) $10x - 2 = 18$

    (I) $-5x - 13 = -38$

3. (N) $20 = 7x - 8$

    (M) $8 = 3x - 1$

4. (H) $8x - 2 = 22$

    (G) $11x - 54 = 1$

5. (C) $100 = 10x - 20$

    (P) $6x - 32 = 4$

6. (R) $30 = 5x - 15$

    (U) $14x - 3 = 25$

7. (I) $17x - 33 = 18$

    (O) $15x - 10 = 140$

8. (T) $30 = 6x - 36$

    (S) $20x - 41 = 199$

9. (B) $9x - 65 = 7$

    (D) $-90 = 4x - 10$

10. (V) $-25 = 5x - 5$

    (Y) $-32 = 8x - 32$

Answer: _____

Name: Date: Class:

SUPREME JUSTICE

In 1967, who became the first African-American to serve on the United States Supreme Court?

Solve for x. Write the exercise number in front of the corresponding answer listed in the grid. To spell out the answer to the question, refer to the grid and write the code letter that corresponds to the exercise number given.

 Tip: When terms containing the same variable are on both sides of the equation, add or subtract the "like terms" to get them on the same side. For example,
$4x = 2x + 36 \rightarrow 4x - 2x = 2x - 2x + 36 \rightarrow 2x = 36 \rightarrow x = 18$.

1. $3x = 6x + 45$

2. $24x + 38 = -14x$

3. $29x = 23x - 42$

4. $30x = 180 - 30x$

5. $8x = 18 - x$

6. $5x + 18 = -4x$

7. $11x = 8x + 21$

8. $32x - 14 = 18$

9. $20x = 24x + 16$

10. $60x + 153 = 9x$

11. $9 - 30x = -42 - 27x$

12. $5x + 21 = -2x - 14$

13. $4x - 10 = -4x + 22$

14. $x - 10 = 5x + 14$

15. $x - 14 = -2 - x$

16. $28 + 10x = 6x - 4$

17. $8x - 92 = 2x - 2$

18. $4x + 93 = -3x + 9$

19. $17 - 9x = -6x - 22$

20. $21x + 100 = 11x - 10$

Code Letter	Exercise #	Answer
A		−7
B		−12
C		−15
D		−8
E		−2
F		17
G		−4
H		−11
I		4
L		13
M		2
N		3
O		−5
P		15
Q		6
R		7
S		−1
T		1
U		−6
Y		−3

Answer:

___ ___ ___ ___ ___ ___ ___ ___ ___ ___ ___ ___ ___ ___ ___

8   20   14   7   9   12   12   16   5   3   7   2   20   3   19   19

Name: Date: Class:

STARRY SKY

What is the name of the last star in the handle of the Little Dipper (also know as the Little Bear)? Hint: It's another name for the North Star.

Solve the problems in numerical order, and find the matching solutions in the list given. Use the corresponding letters to spell out the answer to the question.

 Tip: When calculating a problem that include parenthesis, don't forget to use the distributive property before solving for x. For example,
$5(2x - 3) = 7x \rightarrow 10x - 15 = 7x \rightarrow -15 = -3x \rightarrow 5 = x.$

1. $2(4x + 1) = 10$ 2. $5(x - 5) = x(14 - 4)$

3. $3(10x - 2) = -4(-7x + 11)$ 4. $5(x - 1) = (x + 3)$

 5. $-3(x + 2) = 12$

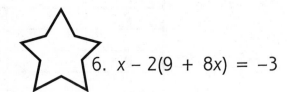 6. $x - 2(9 + 8x) = -3$

 7. $5(2x + 8) = -4(x - 3)$

(P) $x = 1$	(O) $x = -5$	(R) $x = -6$	(R) $x = 3$
(H) $x = -7$	(A) $x = 2$	(L) $x = -19$	(S) $x = -2$
(T) $x = 11$	(I) $x = -1$	(E) $x = 9$	(B) $x = 21$

Answer: _____

ame: _____ Date: _____ Class: _____

ASTONISHING ASTRONAUT

What do astronauts receive when they do their homework?

Solve the following equations for x in terms of y. Draw a line connecting each problem in Column A to its answer in Column B. In front of each exercise number, write the letter representing the answer. Read down the column of written letters to discover the answer to the fun riddle.

 Tip: When simplifying a literal equation, one that includes two or more different variables, you may solve for any one of its variables. For example,
$4y + 2x = 10 \rightarrow 2x = 10 - 4y \rightarrow x = 5 - 2y.$

Column A

_____ 1. $x + y = -2$

_____ 2. $x - y = -6$

_____ 3. $y - x = -5$

_____ 4. $3y + x = 10$

_____ 5. $7y + x = 11$

_____ 6. $3y - x = -8$

_____ 7. $2x - 4y = 6$

_____ 8. $9y - 3x = 12$

_____ 9. $11y - x = -9$

Column B

S. $x = -7y + 11$

R. $x = 7y + 11$

O. $x = y - 6$

U. $x = -y + 6$

R. $x = 3y - 4$

T. $x = 3y + 8$

S. $x = -3y - 8$

D. $x = -3y + 10$

W. $x = 3y + 10$

S. $x = 11y + 9$

L. $x = y + 5$

G. $x = -y - 2$

A. $x = 2y + 3$

S. $x = -2y - 3$

Answer: _____

th

Name: _____   Date: _____   Class: _____

REVIEW WHAT YOU KNOW
ABOUT SOLVING LINEAR EQUATIONS

Simplify the following equations by combining like terms.

1. $3x + 5x - 2x$

2. $4x - 6x - 7x$

3. $-x + 8x - 10x$

4. $2x - 5x + 20x$

5. $-9x - 11x + 15x$

Solve the following equations for x.

6. $3x = 15$

7. $-2x - 9 = 11$

8. $3x + 3 = -36$

9. $x/3 = -12$

10. $-7x - 3x = 20$

11. $-8x + 4 = -4x$

12. $7(1 - x) + 4x = 4x$

13. $10(2x - 4) = -20x$

14. $-7 + 4x = 6x - 5$

15. $(-4 + x)10 = 2x$

Solve the following equations for x in terms of y.

16. $x + y = 9$

17. $-x - 2y = 7$

18. $3x - 6y = -12$

19. $-4y - x = 11$

20. $-2y + 2x = -8$

Answer: _____

Name: Date: Class:

CANDY CRAZE

According to the National Candy Buyers Brands Survey, what candy bar has remained the nation's favorite for many years?

Match each equation to its graph. Write by each exercise number the letter representing the solution. Read down the column of letters to identify the answer to the survey stumper.

 Tip: In a coordinate plane, $x = a$ graphs as a *vertical line* in which the x-coordinate is always a; similarly, $y = b$ graphs as a horizontal line in which the y-coordinate is always b. For example, $x = 3$ is a vertical line that runs through x-coordinate 3 and includes points such as (3, 1), (3, –2), and (3, 7).

_____ 1. $x = -3$

_____ 2. $x = 5$

_____ 3. $y = -4$

_____ 4. $y = -7$

_____ 5. $y = 2$

_____ 6. $y = 6$

_____ 7. $x = -6$

_____ 8. $x = 2$

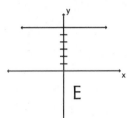

E

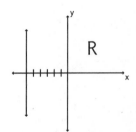

S

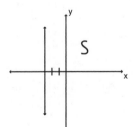

K

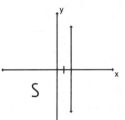

R

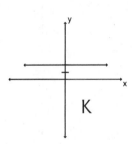

S

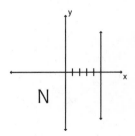

N

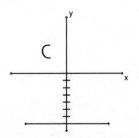

C

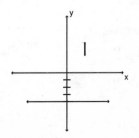

I

Name: _____   Date: _____   Class: _____

CRISSCROSS

What time of day is the best time to see a dentist?

On the large grid, graph each $x = a$ equation. Write next to each graphed line the letter (in parenthesis) associated with the equation. Read the letters on the grid from left to right to discover the first part of the riddle's answer. Repeat the process with each $y = b$ graph, reading downward to reveal the second part of the answer.

 Tip: When drawing graphs, especially those involving linear equations $x = a$ and $y = b$, always label the x-axis, the y-axis, and the line of the equation to avoid possible confusion.

(H) $x = 10$

(Y) $y = -5$

(H) $y = 9$

(T) $x = -5$

(T) $x = 9$

(T) $y = -3$

(R) $y = 0$

(O) $x = 0$

(O) $x = -1$

(U) $y = 8$

Answer: _____

Name: Date: Class:

COLOSSAL CREATURE

What is the largest living thing in the world?

For each exercise, circle the coordinate pair that is a solution to the equation. The letters next to the ten solutions will spell out the two-word answer to the question.

 Tip: To determine if point (x, y) is a solution to a linear equation (i.e., is part of the graph), plug the x-value into the equation and solve for y; if the y-values agree, the point is a solution. For example, point $(2, 1)$ is not a solution to line $y = x + 3$, because substituting 2 for x in the equation yields $y = 5$, not $y = 1$.

1. $y = 2x + 5$ (B) $(2, -1)$ (R) $(-2, 1)$

2. $y = -x - 5$ (E) $(6, -11)$ (A) $(-3, 4)$

3. $y = 7x + 8$ (M) $(1, -2)$ (D) $(-1, 1)$

4. $y = -3x - 6$ (L) $(4, 5)$ (W) $(-2, 0)$

5. $y = -4x + 9$ (O) $(1, 5)$ (G) $(-3, 4)$

6. $y = x + 5$ (O) $(-3, 2)$ (U) $(0, -5)$

7. $2x + 6y = 2$ (H) $(-3, -1)$ (D) $(1, 0)$

8. $-4x - 3y = 5$ (T) $(1, -3)$ (M) $(-3, -2)$

9. $x + 3y = 10$ (Y) $(2, 4)$ (R) $(-2, 4)$

10. $-x - y = 13$ (E) $(-6, -7)$ (S) $(6, 7)$

11. $y = 8x + 2$ (M) $(-1/2, 6)$ (E) $(1/2, 6)$

Answer: _____

Name: _____   Date: _____   Class: _____

LIGHTS, CAMERA, ACTION!

What reissued film in 1997 won a place in the Guinness Book of World Records for selling $98.6 million worth of tickets in its first three weeks?

Determine coordinate points for each equation by completing a "table of values" for x and y. (The x-values in each table are set up for you.) Use the values to help identify the graph of each equation. To spell out the two-word answer to the question, write the letter of each graph in order according to exercise number.

 Tip: To complete a "table of values," plug each x-coordinate value into the equation to solve for the corresponding y-coordinate. For example, if given the equation $y = x + 2$, when $x = 1$, $y = (1) + 2 = 3$; the coordinate point to graph is (1, 3).

1. $y = 3x + 4$

x	y
0	
−1	
1	
−2	

2. $y = x + 2$

x	y
0	
−1	
1	
−2	

3. $y = 2(x - 3)$

x	y
0	
−1	
1	
−2	

4. $2x + 4y = 8$

x	y
0	
−1	
1	
−2	

5. $y = -2x - 1$

x	y
0	
−1	
1	
−2	

6. $y = -x + 6$

x	y
0	
−1	
1	
−2	

7. $y = -(3x - 4)$

x	y
0	
−1	
1	
−2	

8. $-x - 6y = 2$

x	y
0	
−1	
1	
−2	

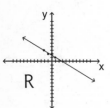

R

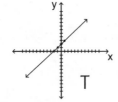

T

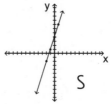

S

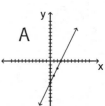

A

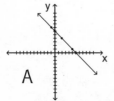

A

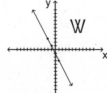

W

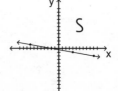

S

R

Answer: _____

MATCH TYPE

This group of animals can live both on land and in water. What is the name of this animal group?

Match each equation to its corresponding graph. Replace each equation number with the letter of the graph to spell out the answer to the question.

Tip: When randomly selecting x-coordinate values for the "table of values," choose numerals that eliminate or simplify the x term in the equation. For example, x values of −1, 0, and 1 are easily calculated into the equation y = 3x − 7 to yield y values of −10, −7, and −4.

1. −5x − y = 2
2. y = x − 5
3. y = −3x + 4
4. y = 3x −2
5. 4x − y = 5

6. −6x − 2y = 10
7. y = −2x + 2
8. y = x + 5
9. −x − y = 1

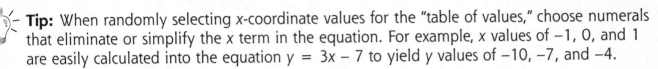
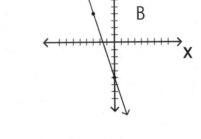
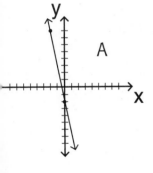
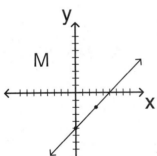
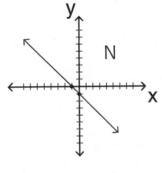
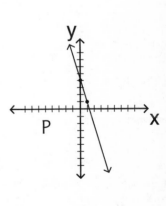
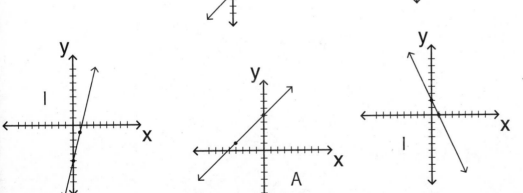

Answer: _____

Name: Date: Class:

— INTERCEPTION —

Which football team has participated in more Super Bowls than any other team, winning five games and losing three?

Determine the *x*- and *y*-intercept of each equation. At the bottom of the page, write the letter of each exercise above its solution to decode the answer to the question.

Tip: To find the *x*-intercept, let $y = 0$ and solve for *x*.
To find the *y*-intercept, let $x = 0$ and solve for *y*. For example,
the *y*-intercept for $2x + 3y = 9$ is (0, 3).

L. $3x - y = -9$

S. $2x + 4y = -12$

B. $6x + 4y = -48$

Y. $-5x - 3y = -45$

C. $-2x + 8y = 24$

D. $-7x - 14y = 28$

L. $-6x - 7y = -42$

O. $9x - 5y = 45$

A. $7x - 3y = 21$

W. $8x - 10y = 40$

S. $x + 13y = -26$

O. $10x + 3y = -30$

A. $2x - 3y = 6$

Answer:

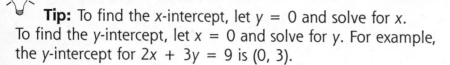

x=−4	x=3	x=−3	x=7	x=3	x=−6		x=−12	x=5	x=5	x=−8	x=−3	x=9	x=−26
y=−2	y=−7	y=9	y=6	y=−2	y=−3		y=3	y=−9	y=−4	y=−12	y=−10	y=15	y=−2

Date: Class:

GRAPH-IC DESIGN

A trapezoid is a quadrilateral in which only two sides are parallel. Can you find the trapezoid in the following dot-to-dot design?

Graph each linear equation using its x- and y-intercept. Identify the two equations whose x- and y-intercepts can be connected together to form a trapezoid.

Tip: When plotting several lines on one graph, be certain to label all points to avoid confusion.

1. $y = -4x - 8$

2. $-5x - 7y = 35$

3. $y = 4x - 2$

4. $2y = 20 - 2x$

5. $4y - 6x = 12$

6. $x + y = 5$

7. $7x - 6y = -42$

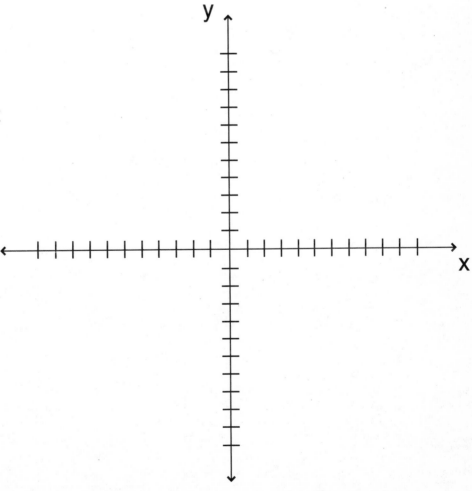

Name: _____   Date: _____   Class: _____

WINTER SLOPES

What two basic types of skiing are practiced on snowy slopes throughout the world?
(Hint: One includes slalom racing and the other includes ski-jumping.)

Find the slope for each pair of coordinate points and identify the answer in the opposite column. Write in front of each exercise number the corresponding letter (in parenthesis). The letters next to odd-numbered problems will spell out one of the answers to the question; the letters next to even-numbered problems will spell out the other.

 Tip: To find the slope of a line given two points, (x_1, x_2) and (y_1, y_2), use the formula $m = (y_2 - y_1)/(x_2 - x_1)$. For example, the slope of a line with points (2, 4) and (3, 6) is $m = (6 - 4)/(3 - 2) \rightarrow m = 2/1 \rightarrow m = 2$.

_____ 1. (2, 3), (4, 2)   (N) 2

_____ 2. (−1, 0), (1, 0)   (L) 3

_____ 3. (−2, 3), (4, 21)   (I) 5

_____ 4. (−6, 5), (−7, 8)   (P) 1

_____ 5. (−2, −2), (−1, −1)   (D) undefined

_____ 6. (8, −4), (−4, 8)   (O) −3

_____ 7. (−3, 5), (3, 8)   (C) 7

_____ 8. (−7, 1), (−7, −1)   (N) 0

_____ 9. (10, 12), (12, 16)   (E) −2

_____10. (9, −8), (13, 12)   (R) −1

_____11. (−1, 2), (0, 0)   (A) −1/2

_____12. (6, −5), (8, 9)   (I) 1/2

Answer: _____

YOUNG MASTER

In 1997, at the age of 21 years and 104 days, this person became the youngest player to win The Masters golf championship. What is this young man's first name?

Use the chart values to answer each question. Round your answers to the nearest hundredth. Find the matching answers in the list given, and write the corresponding letters in front of their exercise numbers. Read down the column of letters to identify the amazing athlete.

Tip: Determining the rate of change is similar to solving for the slope of a line. Use the equation *rate of change = (death$_2$ - death$_1$)/(birth$_2$ - birth$_1$)*.

BIRTH AND DEATH RATES
(rounded to the nearest whole number)

Region	Births (millions per year)	Deaths (millions per year)
Asia	85.0	27.0
Africa	29.0	9.0
South America	13.0	3.0
Europe	9.0	8.0
North America	5.0	3.0

What is the average rate of change of deaths to births between the following regions:

_____ 1. North America and Asia?

_____ 2. North America and South America?

_____ 3. Europe and Africa?

_____ 4. Europe and North America?

_____ 5. Asia and Africa?

Y = 6.3   E = 1.25   R = 2.1   I = 0
T = 0.3   S = 0.9   E = 4.5   M = 3.2
G = 1.3   R = 0.32   H = 0.7   G = 0.05

Name: _____   Date: _____   Class: _____

AMAZING ANIMATION

What animated television series has had 177 shows—and counting—and has become the longest running prime-time cartoon show on television?

Find the slope of the line for each pair of points. Identify whether the line is vertical, horizontal, rising from left to right, or falling from left to right. Circle the letter that represents the correct answer. Read the circled letters downward to identify the answer to the TV trivia.

 Tip: When $m > 0$, the slope is positive and the line rises on the graph from left to right; when $m < 0$, the slope is negative and the line falls on the graph from left to right. When $m = 0$, the line is horizontal; when $m =$ undefined, the line is vertical.

1. (–2, 3), (2, 5)   (T) rises left to right   (O) horizontal   (I) vertical

2. (–1, 1), (2, –2)   (K) rises left to right   (H) falls left to right   (N) horizontal

3. (–2, 0), (–2, 4)   (E) vertical   (A) rises left to right   (B) horizontal

4. (–4, 5), (–4, 5)   (C) vertical   (D) falls left to right   (S) horizontal

5. (5, 6), (7, 12)   (I) rises left to right   (K) falls left to right   (P) vertical

6. (7, –8), (–6, 18)   (R) horizontal   (M) falls left to right   (H) vertical

7. (3, –5), (–3, –5)   (V) falls left to right   (U) rises left to right   (P) horizontal

8. (–9, 10), (–9, –10)   (G) rises left to right   (W) falls left to right   (S) vertical

9. (–1, 2), (–3, 10)   (O) falls left to right   (A) rises left to right   (M) horizontal

10. (0, 0), (–2, –6)   (C) falls left to right   (N) rises left to right   (Y) vertical

11. (4, 8), (–4, –8)   (S) rises left to right   (H) horizontal   (L) vertical

Answer: _____

Date: _____   Class: _____

me: _____

WAVE OF THE FUTURE

Bit, bug, byte, modem, operating system, and software are words used to describe or define which modern convenience?

For each exercise, graph the line that corresponds to the given values. Circle the letter that describes the line. Unscramble the circled letters to spell out the answer to the question.

Tip: Remember that slope $m = a/b = $ rise/run. However, when the slope is negative ($m = -a/b$), move down the y-axis instead of rising up. For example, for point (2, 5) and $m = -2$, move down two positions and over to the right one to reach the next point, (3, 3).

1. (–4, –5), $m = -1/2$

   (I) line rises from left to right

   (U) line falls from left to right

2. (2, 3), $m = 1/3$

   (T) line rises from left to right

   (S) horizontal line

3. (–1, 5), $m = 0$

   (M) horizontal line

   (N) vertical line

4. (0, –2), $m = -4/5$

   (H) line rises from left to right

   (R) line falls from left to right

5. (–3, 7), $m = $ undefined

   (E) vertical line

   (A) horizontal line

6. (5, –1), $m = -1$

   (Q) line rises from left to right

   (P) line falls from left to right

7. (–4, –4), $m = 4$

   (O) line rises from left to right

   (Y) line falls from left to right

8. (0, 3), $m = 1/2$

   (C) line rises from left to right

   (K) line falls from left to right

Answer: _____

th...

Name: _____   Date: _____   Class: _____

MATH MALADY

Why did the math book have to see the doctor?

Identify the graph that corresponds to each pair of point and slope values. Next to each graph, write the letter representing the given values. Read the letters next to the graphs from left to right to reveal the three-word answer to the riddle.

 Tip: Narrow your choices by looking at the slope value *(m)* to determine whether the line rises or falls. Then determine which of the remaining choices corresponds to the given point and slope. For example, point (2, 3) and slope $m = 2$ correspond to a line that rises from the left to right and includes point (2, 3).

R. (–2, 3), $m = 3$
E. (–6, –5), $m = 6$
A. (–2, 3), $m = 1/3$
P. (–5, –6), $m = –6$
L. (4, –1), $m = 2$
T. (–3, –1), $m = 1$
D. (4, –1), $m = –2$

M. (–3, 1), $m = –1$
I. (3, –5), $m = 1/4$
B. (0, –2), $m = 0$
O. (3, –5), $m = –4$
H. (–2, 0), $m = $ undefined
S. (0, –4), $m = 1/4$

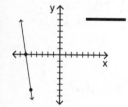 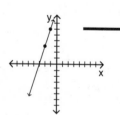 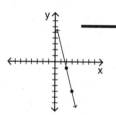 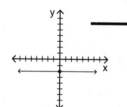 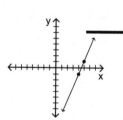

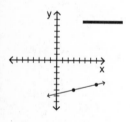 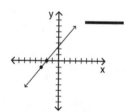 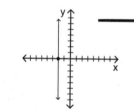 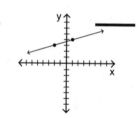 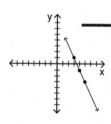

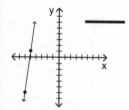 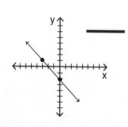 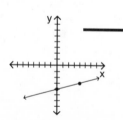

Answer: _____

ne: Date: Class:

STATE YOUR FACTS

This state produced eight future United States presidents and was the birthplace of Thomas A. Edison. It also introduced the world to ice-cream cones. Which state is this?

Change each of the following equations into the slope-intercept form, and identify the slope (m) and the y-intercept (b). Shade in the grid boxes that contain your answers. Read across the remaining unshaded boxes to spell out the answer to the question.

Tip: When changing an equation to the slope-intercept form $(y = mx + b)$, multiply by the reciprocal to eliminate the value in front of the y variable. For example,
$4x + 2y = 6 \rightarrow 2y = 6 - 4x \rightarrow (1/2)2y = (1/2)6 - (1/2)4x \rightarrow y = 3 - 2x.$

1. $3x - 4y = 12$

2. $-2x - 5y = 20$

3. $x + y = -3$

4. $5x - 6y = 30$

5. $7x - 4y = 16$

6. $-8x + 3y = 12$

7. $10x - 2y = 12$

8. $-11x + 11y = -22$

9. $-2x + 9y = 18$

10. $x - 3y = -21$

11. $-6x + y = 10$

12. $x - y = -13$

Y $b = -5$ $m = 5/6$	O $b = 8$ $m = -9$	J $b = -6$ $m = 5$	P $b = -3$ $m = 3/4$
T $b = 7$ $m = 1/3$	U $b = 13$ $m = 1$	N $b = -4$ $m = 7/4$	H $b = -7$ $m = 4$
I $b = 1$ $m = -2$	L $b = 2$ $m = 2/9$	M $b = -3$ $m = -1$	V $b = -4$ $m = -2/5$
R $b = 10$ $m = 6$	A $b = 4$ $m = 8/3$	O $b = -10$ $m = -1$	S $b = -2$ $m = 1$

Answer: _____

Name: Date: Class:

INTRIGUING INVENTION

In 1972, Norman Buschnel of the United States invented a fun-filled gadget that led to a booming business and a favorite pastime for kids all over the world. What was the invention?

Use the slope and y-intercept from each equation to help identify the corresponding graph. Write next to each graph the letter (in parenthesis) from the matching equation. Read the letters by the graphs from left to right to identify the answer to the question.

 Tip: When equations are written in slope-intercept form, $y = mx + b$, the y-intercept (b) is the point at which $x = 0$. For example, when $y = 4x - 8$, the y-intercept is -8 and the corresponding point is $(0, -8)$.

(E) $y = 2x + 3$ (A) $y = -3x + 1$ (M) $y = 7x - 8$
(E) $y = -x - 1$ (G) $y = 2x - 5$ (V) $y = -3x - 2$
(O) $y = -2x - 2$ (I) $y = -x$ (D) $y = -1/2x + 4$

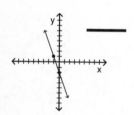 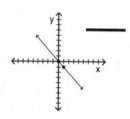 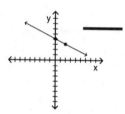 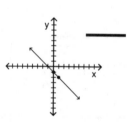 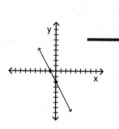

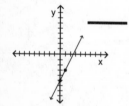 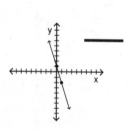 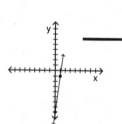 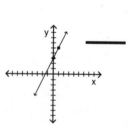

Answer: _____

Date: Class:

me:

ASTONISHING APPLE

In 1994, in Hood River, Oregon, the Hanners family grew the largest apple ever recorded. Over how many pounds did this huge fruit weigh?

On a separate piece of paper, graph the following equations by using the values for slope and y-intercept. Count the number of graphs that pass through only two quadrants—your total will equal the answer to the trivia question.

 Tip: Be aware that two lines may have the same y-intercept, but still graph differently. For example, the equations $y = 6x + 5$ and $y = 3x + 5$ both intersect the y-axis at (0, 5), but the first equation has a slope twice as steep as the second.

1. $y = 2x$

2. $y = -x - 4$

3. $y = x + 3$

4. $y = -7x + 2$

5. $y = -1/6x + 6$

6. $y = 5x - 5$

7. $y = 2/3x - 1$

8. $y = -x$

9. $y = -3x - 7$

10. $y = x$

11. $y = -3/4x + 5$

12. $y = 6x - 2$

Answer: _____

th...

Name: Date: Class:

REVIEW WHAT YOU KNOW
ABOUT GRAPHING LINEAR EQUATIONS

Using a table of values, graph the following one- and two-variable graphs.

1. $x = -1$

2. $y = 5$

3. $3x + 4y = 12$

4. $-2x + 3y = -6$

5. $x - 6y = 12$

Graph the following lines using x- and y-intercepts.

6. $4x + 5y = -20$

7. $-2x - 4y = 12$

8. $3x - 6y = -18$

9. $-4x + 7y = -28$

10. $8x - 3y = -24$

Find the slope of the line passing through each pair of coordinate points. Classify each line, according to its slope, as rising from left to right, falling from left to right, horizontal, or vertical.

11. $(0, 4)(9, -5)$

12. $(-3, 6)(-3, -6)$

13. $(-1, -7)(-2, -12)$

14. $(-9, -10)(-8, -10)$

15. $(2, 3)(-6, -13)$

Write the following equations in slope-intercept form. Identify the slope and y-intercept in each equation. Then draw the graph of each equation.

16. $3x - 6y = 12$

17. $2x + 4y = -16$

18. $-x + y = -7$

19. $-7x - y = 9$

20. $8x - 4y = -40$

POSITIVE THINKING

What is one of the best ways to succeed?

Write the equation of each line given its slope *(m)* and y-intercept *(b)*. Write the exercise number in front of the corresponding answer listed in the grid. To spell out the answer at the bottom of the page, refer to the grid and write the code letter that corresponds to the exercise number given.

 Tip: When plugging *m* and *b* values into the equation $y = mx + b$, don't forget to include negative symbols when given. For example, when $m = -4$ and $b = -6$, the equation is $y = -4x - 6$.

1. $m = 2, b = -5$

2. $m = 1/3, b = 2$

3. $m = -4, b = -3$

4. $m = -1/2, b = 8$

5. $m = -3, b = -4$

6. $m = -1/3, b = -2$

7. $m = -5, b = 2$

8. $m = -10, b = -9$

9. $m = 8, b = -1/2$

10. $m = 2, b = 1/3$

11. $m = -1, b = 0$

12. $m = 1, b = -1$

13. $m = 0, b = -5$

14. $m = -1, b = -1$

Code Letter	Exercise #	Answer
A		$y = -x$
C		$y = 8x - 1/2$
D		$y = -x - 1$
E		$y = 1/3x + 2$
F		$y = 2x + 1/3$
I		$y = 2x - 5$
L		$y = -5x + 2$
M		$y = -1/2x + 8$
N		$y = x - 1$
O		$y = -10x - 9$
R		$y = -4x - 3$
T		$y = -1/3x - 2$
U		$y = -5$
Y		$y = -3x - 4$

Answer:

___ ___ ___ ___ ___   ___ ___ ___ ___   ___ ___ ___ ___
9   7   2   11   3   5   8   13   3   4   1   12   14

            ___ ___ ___ ___ ___ ___ '___ !!
             8   10   9   11   12   6

Name: Date: Class:

FAST TRACK

In 1948, the first stored-program computer was invented. In 1981, the first portable computer was made. In 1991, IBM released this kind of computer to the public. What is it called?

Write the equation of each line given its slope *m* and one coordinate point. Circle the *y*-intercept value in each equation. To spell out the answer to the question, match the letter of each problem to the corresponding *y*-intercept value given.

 Tip: First use the *m* value and point (x, y) in the equation $y = mx + b$ to solve for *b*. Then plug the *b* and *m* values (not the point values) back into slope-intercept form. For example, if $m = 2$ and a point on the line is $(-1, 3)$, then $3 = (2)(-1) + b \rightarrow 5 = b$, and the equation of the line is $y = 2x + 5$.

I. $(3, -4)$, $m = 2$

N. $(10, 4)$, $m = 1$

U. $(-1, -2)$, $m = 5$

T. $(4, -2)$, $m = -7$

E. $(-8, 6)$, $m = 4$

P. $(-1, -1)$, $m = 6$

M. $(8, 2)$, $m = -1$

C. $(-6, 0)$, $m = -1/2$

P. $(-3, 5)$, $m = 9$

Answer:

$\overline{32}$ $\overline{38}$ $\overline{-6}$ $\overline{26}$ $\overline{-10}$ $\overline{3}$ $\overline{10}$ $\overline{5}$ $\overline{-3}$

me: Date: Class:

PLANET INTELLECT

What do planets like to read?

Draw a line connecting each set of values in Column A to its equation in Column B. To spell out the two-word answer to the riddle, write in front of the equations in Column B the corresponding letters from Column A.

Tip: Plug the values for b and m into the slope-intercept equation, $y = mx + b$. Change the Column B equations into slope-intercept form and compare results.

Column A

O. $b = -3$, $m = 3/4$

T. $b = 2$, $m = 2/9$

M. $b = -6$, $m = 5$

E. $b = -4$, $m = -2/5$

B. $b = -2$, $m = 1$

S. $b = -5$, $m = 5/6$

O. $b = -3$, $m = -1$

C. $b = -4$, $m = 7/4$

K. $b = 7$, $m = 1/3$

O. $b = 10$, $m = 6$

Column B

____ $7x - 4y = 16$

____ $3x - 4y = 12$

____ $10x - 2y = 12$

____ $-2x - 5y = 20$

____ $-2x + 9y = 18$

____ $-11x + 11y = -22$

____ $x + y = -3$

____ $-6x + y = 10$

____ $x - 3y = -21$

____ $5x - 6y = 30$

Answer: _____

th...

Name: Date: Class:

GREEK GAMES

The first Olympic Games, played in Greece in 776 B.C., featured only one event. What was it?

For each set of ordered pairs, write the equation of the corresponding line. Find the matching answers in the list given, and write the corresponding letters in front of their exercise numbers. Read down the column of letters to identify the Olympic event.

 Tip: First solve for m by using the formula $m = (y_2 - y_1) / (x_2 - x_1)$. Next, solve for b by using the m value and one of the ordered pairs. Last, use the b and m values to write the equation of the line. For example, when given (2, 3) and (4, 7):

$m = (7 - 3) / (4 - 2) \rightarrow 2$; $b = 7 - (2)(4) \rightarrow -1$; and the equation of the line is $y = 2x - 1$.

_____ 1. (3, –2), (4, 0)

_____ 2. (1, 2), (3, –2)

_____ 3. (8, 4), (10, –2)

_____ 4. (–3, –5), (6, 13)

_____ 5. (7, –4), (4, 5)

_____ 6. (0, 0), (–7, 14)

_____ 7. (–1, –1), (4, 14)

_____ 8. (–3, 0), (6, 27)

(R) $y = -3x + 17$

(E) $y = 3x + 9$

(F) $y = 2x - 8$

(C) $y = 3x + 2$

(O) $y = -2x + 4$

(T) $y = 2x + 1$

(A) $y = -2x$

(O) $y = -3x + 28$

© Good Apple GA16

Name: _____   Date: _____   Class: _____

SMART BUTTER

Where does smart butter go?

For each pair of points, write the corresponding slope-intercept equation. To reveal the riddle's answer at the bottom of the page, write the letter of each problem above its y-intercept.

 Tip: When asked to write the equation of a line $y = mx + b$ that includes points (x_1, y_1) and (x_2, y_2), remember to solve for m and then b by using the equations $m = (y_2 - y_1) / (x_2 - x_1)$ and $b = y - mx$.

O. (4, 0) (−3, 7) _____

R. (−6, 8) (−7, 4) _____

L. (5, 10) (2, 4) _____

N. (−1, −2) (−7, 10) _____

R. (0, −11) (8, 13) _____

H. (8, 9) (−12, 9) _____

L. (4, −5) (−1, 15) _____

O. (6, 3) (7, 4) _____

O. (−10, −12) (−15, 3) _____

Answer:

___ ___ ___ ___ ___   ___ ___ ___ ___
 9   4   −4 −42 32   −11 −3   0   11

Name: _____   Date: _____   Class: _____

SIZING UP SAND

The world's biggest desert, measuring 3.5 million square miles, is found in Africa. What is the name of this desert?

Match each equation to its graph. (Hint: Compare slope and y-intercept values.) Write next to the graph the letter representing its equation. Read the letters from left to right to identify the name of the desert.

 Tip: The y-intercept is the point at which the graphed line crosses the y-axis. The slope m is the distance (m = rise/run) between two points on the line.

(H) $y = -2x - 1$ (S) $y = -x + 6$ (A) $y = 4x - 2$ (R) $y = 5x - 4$
(A) $y = 1/2x - 1$ (A) $y = -x - 6$

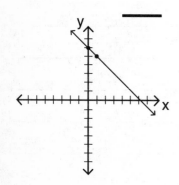 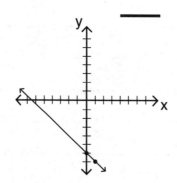 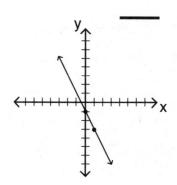

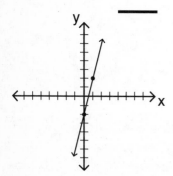 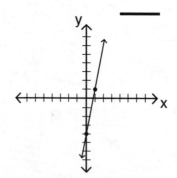 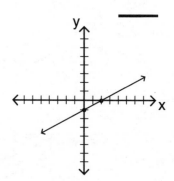

Answer: _____

Name: Date: Class:

LET'S GET TO THE POINT

The "lead" in pencils is not really lead. What is it?

Match each slope-intercept equation in Column A to its standard-form equation in Column B. Write in front of each exercise number the letter representing the solution. Use the letters from the even-numbered problems to spell out the answer to the question.

 Tip: Isolate x and y terms on the left side of the equation to transform slope-intercept equations into standard form $Ax + By = C$. Note that a linear equation can have more than one standard form. For example, if you multiply $-3x + 2y = 6$ by -1, you would get $3x - 2y = -6$, which is still in standard form.

Column A

_____ 1. $y = -3x + 3$

_____ 2. $y = -x - 6$

_____ 3. $y = 1/7x + 4$

_____ 4. $y = 5x - 8$

_____ 5. $y = -4x + 6$

_____ 6. $y = 7x + 9$

_____ 7. $-3x - 4y - 20 = -18$

_____ 8. $5x + 6y + 4 = 0$

_____ 9. $-x - 10y - 32 = -12$

_____ 10. $2x - 7y - 14 = -21$

_____ 11. $8x - 4y = 12 + 8$

_____ 12. $-9x - 9y - 9 = 17$

_____ 13. $7x + 6y - 3 = -4$

_____ 14. $-5x + 2y - 16 = 0$

_____ 15. $-12x + 11y - 13 = 4$

_____ 16. $3x - 2y - 6 + 4 = 12$

Column B

(P) $5x + 6y = -4$

(A) $8x - 4y = 20$

(E) $3x - 2y = 14$

(G) $x + y = -6$

(L) $4x + y = 6$

(P) $-x + 7y = 28$

(T) $-5x + 2y = 16$

(T) $-x - 10y = 20$

(I) $-9x - 9y = 26$

(C) $3x + y = 3$

(R) $-5x + y = -8$

(O) $-3x - 4y = 2$

(A) $-7x + y = 9$

(H) $2x - 7y = -7$

(A) $-12x + 11y = 17$

(E) $7x + 6y = -1$

Answer: _____

Good Apple GA1687

Name: Date: Class:

LET THE MUSIC PLAY

This pop-music songwriter, born in 1942, has had 32 number-one singles in the United States and 28 in the United Kingdom.
Who is this famous musician?

For each exercise, write the standard-form equation of a line that includes the values given. Shade in the grid boxes that contain your solutions. Read across the remaining unshaded boxes to spell out the answer to the question.

 Tip: Put b, m, and point values in the slope-intercept form $y = mx + b$, and then transform the equation into the standard form $Ax + By = C$. Remember: $m = (y_2 - y_1) / (x_2 - x_1)$ and $b = y - mx$.

1. $b = 4$, $m = -10$

2. $(-3,-2)$, $m = 3$

3. $(-1,-1)$, $(-4,-7)$

4. $(0,-9)$, $(-3,12)$

5. $b = -7$, $m = 8$

6. $(-2,-4)$, $m = -6$

7. $(-4,5)$, $(9,-21)$

8. $(-3,7)$, $m = -1$

9. $b = -5$, $m = 8$

10. $(4,8)$, $(2,10)$

11. $b = -3$, $m = 1$

B	P	E	A	S	U
$7x + y = -9$	$3x + 4y = 11$	$x + y = 4$	$-2x - 5y = 12$	$10x + y = 4$	$8x - 9y = -1$
R	L	Y	W	M	C
$-3x + y = 7$	$x - 3y = 21$	$-8x + y = -7$	$-8x + y = -5$	$4x + 8y = 13$	$-2x + 2y = 3$
C	O	V	A	G	R
$-6x - 7y = 2$	$-x + y = -3$	$6x + y = -16$	$-13x - y = 10$	$-2x + y = 1$	$-x + 5y = 4$
T	D	N	E	K	Y
$2x + y = 1$	$x + y = 12$	$-10x - y = 4$	$7x - y = 9$	$2x + y = -3$	$5x + y = -13$

Answer: _____

ELDERLY ANIMAL

Which animal can live for up to 200 years?

For each exercise, write the point-slope equation of a line that includes the given values. Write the exercise number in front of the corresponding answer listed in the grid. To spell out the answer at the bottom of the page, refer to the grid and then write the corresponding code letter above the exercise number given.

 Tip: To write an equation in point-slope form, plug the values for the slope m and a point (x_1, y_1) into the equation $y - y_1 = m(x - x_1)$. For example, the point-slope equation of a line that includes point (2, 4) and $m = 3$ is $y - 4 = 3(x - 2)$.

1. $(-4, 5)$, $m = 4$

2. $(7, 8)$, $m = -2$

3. $(-1, -4)$, $m = 2$

4. $(3, 9)$, $m = 7$

5. $(-4, 6)$, $m = 3$

6. $(-7, -8)$, $m = -2$

7. $(-3, 9)$, $m = -7$

8. $(-8, 3)$, $m = -3$

9. $(-2, -6)$, $m = 6$

10. $(-7, -9)$, $m = 5$

11. $(-3, -3)$, $m = -2$

12. $(-10, -9)$, $m = 8$

13. $(10, 9)$, $m = -8$

14. $(-3, 3)$, $m = 3$

15. $(2, 6)$, $m = -6$

Code Letter	Exercise #	Answer
A		$y - 5 = 4(x + 4)$
D		$y + 9 = 5(x + 7)$
E		$y - 6 = 3(x + 4)$
F		$y - 3 = -3(x + 8)$
G		$y - 9 = -7(x + 3)$
H		$y - 6 = -6(x - 2)$
I		$y - 9 = 7(x - 3)$
L		$y + 3 = -2(x + 3)$
M		$y - 3 = 3(x + 3)$
N		$y - 8 = -2(x - 7)$
O		$y + 8 = -2(x + 7)$
P		$y + 6 = 6(x + 2)$
R		$y + 9 = 8(x + 10)$
S		$y + 4 = 2(x + 1)$
T		$y - 9 = -8(x - 10)$

Answer:

___ ___ ___ ___ ___   ___ ___ ___ ___ ___ ___ ___ ___
 7   4   1   2   13   13   6   12   13   6   4   3   5

Name: Date: Class:

REVIEW WHAT YOU KNOW
ABOUT WRITING LINEAR EQUATIONS

Write the slope-intercept equation of each line given its slope and y-intercept.

1. $m = 3, b = -4$

2. $m = -1, b = 5$

3. $m = -6, b = -7$

4. $m = 8, b = 12$

5. $m = -2, b = -9$

Write the slope-intercept equation of each line given two of its coordinate points.

6. $(9, 6)(5, -2)$

7. $(-2, 1)(3, 6)$

8. $(4, 5)(2, -1)$

9. $(-7, 2)(5, -22)$

10. $(-1, 1)(3, -11)$

Change the following slope-intercept equations into standard form.

11. $y = -2x + 5$

12. $y = 3x - 7$

13. $y = -5x - 9$

14. $4x - y - 10 = 0$

15. $x + 2y - 6 = 0$

Write the point-slope equation of a line given its slope and one coordinate point.

16. $(-3, 4), m = -8$

17. $(-1, 2), m = 10$

18. $(5, -6), m = -3$

19. $(-8, -2), m = 7$

20. $(9, -10), m = -6$

Name: _____   Date: _____   Class: _____

CREATIVE COMBINATIONS

What happens when certain animals cross paths? See if you can figure out these creative combinations!

For each exercise, complete the table by substituting each *x* value into the equation and solving for *y*. Find the code letters that match the *y* values, and write the letters in the space provided to spell out the answer to the puzzler.

 Tip: Solve what's in between the absolute-value sign first. Remember that an absolute-value sign changes a negative number to a positive. For example,
$-5|3 - 7| + 8 \rightarrow -5|-4| + 8 \rightarrow -5(4) + 8 \rightarrow -12$.

−10	−4	12	3	0	−8	−2	4	−5	−1	−3	−6	1	−19
A	B	C	E	F	I	L	M	N	O	P	R	T	W

1. What do you get when you cross a lion and a zebra?

   $y = -2|x - 1| + 2$ Answer: _____

x	−1	−4	−2	5	−5
y					

2. What do you get when you cross a llama and a gopher?

   $y = -|x + 5| + 3$ Answer: _____

x	0	−9	8	−8	−5	4
y						

3. What do you get when you cross a walrus and an alligator?

   $y = |x + 1| - 20$ Answer: _____

x	0	−11	−13	−22	−24	13
y						

Name: _____   Date: _____   Class: _____

RICHIE RICH

What family in the United States owns a well-known chain of discount stores and is one of the richest families in the world?

Solve for x. Circle the letter that is next to the solution to each equation. Read the circled letters downward to reveal the two-word answer to the question.

 Tip: To solve for x in an equation $|x + b| = c$, isolate the absolute-value term and then set $x + b = c$ and $x + b = -c$. For example, $2 + |x + 3| = 8 \rightarrow |x + 3| = 6 \rightarrow x + 3 = 6$ and $x + 3 = -6 \rightarrow x = 3$ and $x = -9$.

1. $|x - 2| = 5$ (D) $x = 3, 7$ (W) $x = -3, 7$

2. $|x + 7| = 10$ (A) $x = 3, -17$ (U) $x = -3, -17$

3. $|x - 4| = 1$ (L) $x = 5, 3$ (M) $x = -5, 3$

4. $3 + |x - 1| = 6$ (S) $x = -4, 2$ (T) $x = 4, -2$

5. $-7 + |x - 3| = 9$ (Y) $x = 1, 5$ (O) $x = 19, -13$

6. $-|x - 6| = -8$ (N) $x = -2, 14$ (M) $x = 2, -14$

7. $-10 + |x + 2| = 7$ (F) $x = 15, -19$ (G) $x = -15, 19$

8. $3 - |x - 5| = -2$ (E) $x = 4, 6$ (A) $x = 0, 10$

9. $|x + 1| - 10 = 11$ (M) $x = 20, -22$ (K) $x = 0, 3$

10. $|2x + 4| = 8$ (O) $x = 2, 6$ (I) $x = 2, -6$

11. $|3x - 9| - 12 = 3$ (S) $x = 8, 2$ (L) $x = 8, -2$

12. $3 + |5x - 2| + 6 = 17$ (Y) $x = -6/5, 2$ (R) $x = -6/5, -2$

Answer: _____

Name: Date: Class:

ANIMAL MIX-UP

What do you get when you cross a skunk and a whale? Hint: It can be used to solve math problems.

For each equation, calculate the vertex of the corresponding graph. Shade in the grid boxes that contain your solutions. Read across the remaining unshaded boxes to spell out the answer to the question.

 Tip: When given the equation $y = a|x + b| + c$, you can determine the coordinates of the vertex of the corresponding graph by setting $x + b = 0$ and solving for x; the value of y is the same as the value of c. For example, if a graph has the equation $y = |x + 1| - 6$, then $y = c = -6$ and $x + 1 = 0 \rightarrow x = -1$; the vertex is point $(-1, -6)$.

1. $y = |x - 2| + 6$
2. $y = -2|x + 3| - 4$
3. $y = 4|x + 5| - 7$
4. $y = |x - 1|$
5. $y = |x + 9| - 9$
6. $y = -6|x - 8|$
7. $y = |x| - 2$
8. $y = -10|x + 4| - 5$

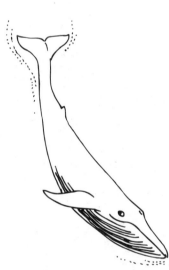

9. $y = -|x - 5|$
10. $y = |x|$
11. $y = |x + 6| - 6$
12. $y = -5|x| - 8$
13. $y = |x + 1| - 1$
14. $y = 7|x + 7| - 7$
15. $y = -8|x + 8|$

A (−4, −5)	B (0, 0)	J (−5, −7)	S (3, 2)	R (−8, 0)
G (0, −2)	P (−1, −1)	L (2, 6)	C (9, −9)	U (5, 0)
M (0, −8)	A (3, 4)	V (−3, −4)	W (−6, −6)	L (9, 0)
T (8, 0)	H (−7, −7)	E (1, 1)	N (1, 0)	K (−9, −9)

Answer: _____

Name: Date: Class:

SIZABLE CITY

This country includes the world's largest city, an area that houses over 25 million people—1/5 of the country's population. What is the name of the city and country?

Match each equation to its corresponding graph. Write in front of the exercise number the letter of the matching graph to spell out the two-word answer to the population puzzler.

 Tip: First use the equations $x + b = 0$ and $y = c$ to calculate the vertex point. Then compare the calculated value to the various graphed values to find the match.

_____ 1. $y = -|x - 3| + 4$ _____ 6. $y = -|x|$

_____ 2. $y = -2|x| - 3$ _____ 7. $y = -7|x - 3| - 2$

_____ 3. $y = |x - 5|$ _____ 8. $y = 9|x + 6| + 4$

_____ 4. $y = 6|x + 7| + 3$ _____ 9. $y = 10|x - 2|$

_____ 5. $y = -5|x - 1| - 1$ _____ 10. $y = -1/2|x - 8| + 1$

A 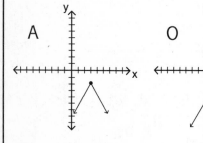   O   K 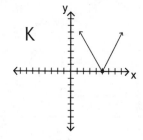   A 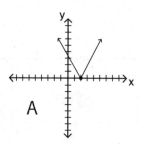   N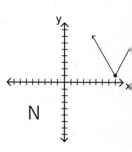

T 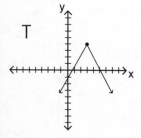   Y 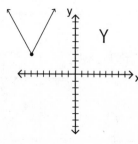   P 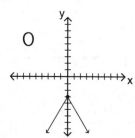   O 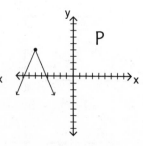   J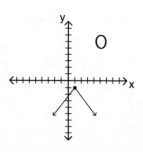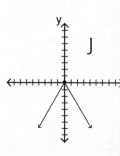

Name: _____   Date: _____   Class: _____

ABSOLUTE WINNERS

The San Francisco 49ers and the Dallas Cowboys share the world record for the greatest number of Super Bowl wins. How many Super Bowl rings has each team received?

On a separate piece of graph paper, draw the V-graph of each absolute-value equations. Count the number of graphs that open up—your total will equal the "winning" answer to the puzzler.

Tip: First calculate and graph the vertex point. Then set up and plot a table of values: Randomly select four x values—two greater than and two less than the x-coordinate of the vertex—and plug each one into the equation to solve for the corresponding y. For example, if a graph has vertex (–2, 3), x values to select include –4, –3, 0, and 1.

1. $y = -3|x - 2| + 4$

2. $y = |x + 3| - 5$

3. $y = 5|x + 4| - 6$

4. $y = -|x| + 7$

5. $y = 2|x - 1|$

6. $y = -2/3|x - 3| - 2$

7. $y = |x + 2| - 2$

8. $y = 1/4|x + 1| + 3$

9. $y = -5|x|$

10. $y = -1/2|x + 4| - 4$

Answer: _____

Good Apple GA1687

Name: _____   Date: _____   Class: _____

PUBLIC RECORD

The Palace of Governors, built in the year 1610, is the oldest public building in the United States. In which city and state is it found?

Solve for each x and find the matching solution in the list given. To spell out the two-part answer to the trivia question, write in front of each exercise number the letter (in parenthesis) representing its solution.

 Tip: When solving for a variable in an inequality equation, remember to reverse the inequality sign when you multiply or divide by a negative number. For example, $-3x - 2 > 4 \rightarrow -3x > 6 \rightarrow x < -2$.

_____ 1. $x + 5 > -4$ (F) $x \leq 12$

_____ 2. $x - 3 > -9$ (O) $x > 12$

_____ 3. $7 - x \geq 10$ (N) $x < -9$

_____ 4. $-9 - x \leq -11$ (E) $x > 2$

_____ 5. $-4 + x < 2$ (S) $x > -9$

_____ 6. $-x - 12 \geq -24$ (T) $x \geq 2$

_____ 7. $x - 35 < 42$ (W) $x < -90$

_____ 8. $x + 91 < 82$ (N) $x \leq -3$

_____ 9. $34 - x \geq 23$ (A) $x < 6$

_____ 10. $x + 45 < -45$ (E) $x \leq 11$

_____ 11. $x - 13 \geq 85$ (C) $x \geq -33$

_____ 12. $67 - x < 65$ (A) $x > -6$

_____ 13. $80 + x \leq -12$ (E) $x < 77$

_____ 14. $15 - x > -17$ (M) $x \geq 98$

_____ 15. $-x + -9 \leq 24$ (X) $x \leq -92$

_____ 16. $x - 52 > -40$ (I) $x < 32$

me: Date: Class:

KISS UNDERCOVER

What is the approximate area of the foil wrapper covering a Hershey's Kiss?

Solve for x. Find your answers in the given list, and circle the corresponding letters. Read down columns of circled letters to reveal the three-word answer to the Kiss question.

 Tip: Check your answer to see if the inequality equation holds true. For example, if you calculate $x < 6$ for the equation $-4 + x < 2$, select a value less than 6 (e.g., 5) and substitute it for x in the equation: $-4 + (5) < 2 \rightarrow 1 < 2$, which is a true statement.

1. $3x - 4 < 11$

2. $-5x + 2 \geq -3$

3. $4x + 10 < 50$

4. $-3x + 32 < 53$

5. $9x - 6 \geq 48$

6. $10x - 92 < 18$

7. $-11 - 11x > 33$

8. $3x - 6 \geq 30$

9. $9 - 8x < -55$

10. $8x + 12 < 60$

11. $4 - 7x > -45$

12. $6 - 5x \leq -39$

13. $-2x + 4 > 6$

14. $15 - 17x \leq -19$

15. $80 - 2x < 40$

16. $4 + 30x \geq -146$

Column One
(R) $x < -9$
(F) $x < 5$
(W) $x > -12$
(I) $x \leq 1$
(V) $x < 10$
(D) $x > -11$
(T) $x > 4$
(E) $x > 20$
(H) $x > 14$
(V) $x > 40$

Column Two
(P) $x > -13$
(S) $x \geq -5$
(Q) $x < 11$
(B) $x > -19$
(U) $x < -4$
(L) $x > -3$
(A) $x \geq 12$
(R) $x > 8$
(G) $x > -10$
(E) $x < 6$

Column Three
(U) $x < -4$
(I) $x < 7$
(X) $x > 42$
(N) $x \geq 9$
(C) $x < -1$
(M) $x < -39$
(H) $x \geq 2$
(E) $x > -7$
(N) $x > 35$
(S) $x \geq 6$

Answer: _____

th...

Name: _____ Date: _____ Class: _____

ON THE RIGHT TRACK

How many world track records did Jesse Owens set in one afternoon in 1935?

Solve the following compound inequalities for x. Count the number of answers in which you switched the direction of the inequality symbols—your total will equal the answer to the sports question.

 Tip: When isolating the x term in the middle of the equation, you must perform the same calculations on *both* sides of the inequality. Also remember to reverse the inequality signs when dividing or multiplying by a negative number. For example,

$-8 < 2 - 5x < 7 \rightarrow -8 - 2 < -5x < 7 - 2 \rightarrow -10 < -5x < 5 \rightarrow$
$-10(-1/5) > x > 5(-1/5) \rightarrow 2 > x > -1$ or $-1 < x < 2.$

1. $-4 < 2x - 6 < 5$

2. $-7 > 8x + 9 > -15$

3. $6 \geq 5x - 4 \geq 1$

4. $22 > -6x - 2 > 4$

5. $-2 < 4x - 8 < 10$

6. $-7 \geq 6 - 13x \geq -33$

7. $8 > 9x - 1 > -28$

8. $-3 \leq 7x - 17 < 18$

9. $-10 < 4 - 2x < -8$

10. $25 > 45 - 5x > 15$

11. $-3 > 7 - 10x \geq -33$

12. $21 > 24 - 3x > 15$

Answer: _____

Name: Date: Class:

TASTY GEOGRAPHY

The world's largest chocolate and cocoa factory is found in a city called Hershey. In which state is this city found?

Match each compound inequality to its graph, and then circle the corresponding letter. Read down the list of circled letters to spell out the answer the question.

 Tip: Graph the two end marks first, and then fill in the rest of the graph. Remember to use an open dot when graphing a < or > endpoint and a solid dot for a ≤ or ≥ endpoint.

1. $2 \le x \le 3$ (M)   (P)

2. $-7 < x \le 1$ (E)   (I)

3. $-2 < x < 8$ (N)   (R)

4. $-4 \le x \le -1$ (T)   (N)

5. $2 \le x < 6$ (S)   (O)

6. $-5 \le x \le 3$ (W)   (Y)

7. $x < -4$ or $x > 7$ (N)   (L)

8. $x \le -2$ or $x \ge 3$ (V)   (E)

9. $x < -1$ or $x > 3$ (A)   (G)

10. $x \ge 1$ or $x < -4$ (S)   (N)

11. $x > 4$ or $x \le -5$ (I)   (U)

12. $x \ge 5$ or $x \le -6$ (D)   (A)

Answer: _____

Name: Date: Class:

TALL TALENT

When he accepted his Emmy for the television sitcom "Family Ties," he said, "I feel four feet tall!" Who is this well-known actor?

Solve each equation. Identify the graph that matches each solution, and write by the exercise number the corresponding letter (in parenthesis). Read the letters downward to reveal the identity of this TV talent.

 Tip: Remember that $|ax + b| < c$ is equivalent to the equation $-c < ax + b < c$, and $|ax + b| > c$ is equivalent to the pair of equations $ax + b > c$ or $ax + b < -c$. For example, $|3x + 2| < 5$ is the same as $-5 < 3x + 2 < 5$.

___ 1. $|2x - 4| > 6$ ___ 7. $|6 + 2x| \geq 2$

___ 2. $|1 + x| \leq 5$ ___ 8. $|x - 10| < 8$

___ 3. $|4 - x| < 2$ ___ 9. $|4 + 5x| > 14$

___ 4. $|3x - 3| \geq 6$ ___ 10. $|7 - 3x| \geq 2$

___ 5. $|x + 8| > 5$ ___ 11. $|x + 4| < 10$

___ 6. $|10 - 4x| < 2$

I
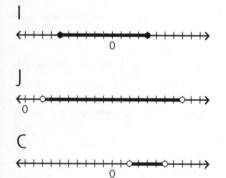

A

E
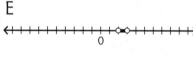

J

H
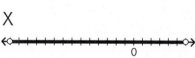

X

C

O

L

F
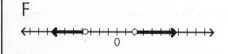

M
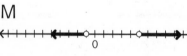
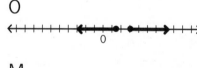

Answer: _____

me: Date: Class:

MONEY MATH

The first U.S. Treasury Secretary, Alexander Hamilton, is pictured on which currency?

For each inequality, write *yes* if the ordered pair is a solution; write *no* if it is not. Count the number of yes answers—your total will equal the dollar-bill value that displays a picture of Alexander Hamilton.

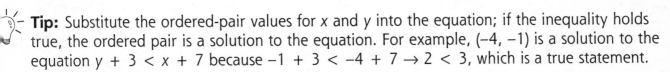 **Tip:** Substitute the ordered-pair values for x and y into the equation; if the inequality holds true, the ordered pair is a solution to the equation. For example, $(-4, -1)$ is a solution to the equation $y + 3 < x + 7$ because $-1 + 3 < -4 + 7 \rightarrow 2 < 3$, which is a true statement.

1. $y < 2x + 3$, $(-2, 0)$

2. $3x - 4y \geq -2$, $(4, -3)$

3. $-5x + 7y \leq 8$, $(-2, -4)$

4. $-x - y < 5$, $(-1, 4)$

5. $8x - 10y \geq 21$, $(4, 1)$

6. $7x - 6y < -5$, $(-2, -5)$

7. $-12x - y > 14$, $(-1, 3)$

8. $9x + 14y \geq -4$, $(-3, 2)$

9. $20x - 15y < 0$, $(2, 3)$

10. $y < -2x - 21$, $(0, -4)$

11. $y > -18x - 11$, $(3, -8)$

12. $-5x - 32y \leq -1$, $(-10, -2)$

13. $y > 17x - 13$, $(-2, 0)$

14. $-23x - 30y < -14$, $(2, -1)$

15. $y \leq 42x + 15$, $(0, 15)$

16. $-x - 14y \geq 14$, $(-10, 3)$

Answer: _____

Name: _____   Date: _____   Class: _____

MATCHING MEASURES

What is the name of the metric measurement that is equivalent to 39.37 inches?

For each exercise, circle the letter of the graph that matches the inequality. Unscramble the circled letters to discover the answer to the question.

 Tip: Set up a "table of values" for the corresponding linear equation (y = mx + b) and compare the (x, y) values to those of the graphed line. If the inequality includes < or > symbols, look for the graph that has a broken line (a ≤ or ≥ graph has a solid line). Finally, select a point from the shaded portion of the graph and determine if the ordered pair is a solution to the equation.

1. $y < 2x + 5$ (E) 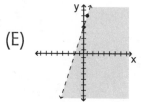   (I)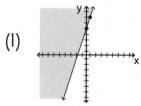

2. $3x - 4y \geq -4$ (G) 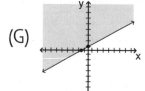   (E)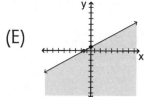

3. $-x - y > 3$ (H) 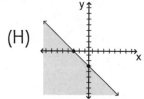   (M)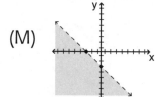

4. $y - 4x \leq 0$ (R) 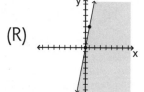   (S)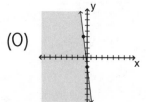

5. $y > -6x - 2$ (O)   (T)

Answer: _____

Name: Date: Class:

RECORD RACE

Richard Petty holds the record for the greatest number of wins at the Daytona 500 car race. How many times has he accomplished this feat?

On a separate piece of paper, graph each inequalities. Count the number of graphs you shaded *above* each line (rather than below)—your total will equal the number of winning races.

 Tip: To graph an inequality equation, first graph the corresponding linear equation $y = mx + b$, drawing a broken line to represent $<$ or $>$ and a solid line to represent $\leq$ or $\geq$. Then select a coordinate point that is above or below the line and use the x and y values in the inequality equation. If the point is a solution, shade that half of the plane; if it is not, shade the other half.

1. $5x - 5y \leq 10$

6. $y \geq -3$

2. $y \geq -4x - 2$

7. $-2x - 5y \geq -10$

3. $x - 2y \geq -4$

8. $-3x - y \leq 2$

4. $y \geq -4$

9. $-x - y \leq -1$

5. $6x - 8y \geq -24$

10. $y \geq -4x - 6$

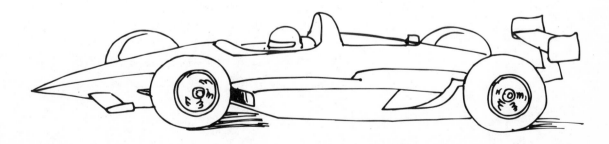

Answer: _____

Name: Date: Class:

REVIEW WHAT YOU KNOW ABOUT ABSOLUTE VALUES & INEQUALITIES

Solve the following absolute-value equations.

1. $|x - 5| = 7$

2. $|x + 3| - 6 = 10$

3. $|4x + 3| - 4 = 8$

4. $3 + |-2x + 9| = 10$

5. $6 + |-x - 5| = 9$

Graph the following absolute-value equations.

6. $y = |x| - 4$

7. $y = |x - 1| + 2$

8. $y = -|x - 3| + 4$

9. $y = |x + 5| - 3$

10. $y = -|x + 2| - 1$

Solve the following inequalities and graph each solution.

11. $x + 6 < 9$

12. $7 - 2x \geq -11$

13. $-6 \leq x - 4 \leq 4$

14. $6 - 2x \geq 20$ or $8 - x \leq 7$

15. $-10 < 6 - 2x < 8$

16. $-14x \geq 28$

17. $-4 < 3 - x < 2$

18. $|x - 3| \leq 4$

19. $|3 + 2x| > 7$

20. $|-x - 3| \leq 1$

Graph the following linear inequalities.

21. $-3x - 2y \leq 6$

22. $-4x + 5y \geq -20$

23. $7x - 3y \leq 21$

24. $-x + y \leq -5$

25. $-2x - 4y \geq 8$

me: Date: Class:

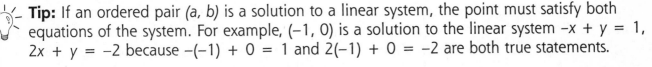

QUADRILATERAL QUESTION

Which geometric shapes are quadrilaterals that have only *one* pair of parallel sides?

For each problem, circle the ordered pair that is a solution to the linear system. Shade in the grid boxes that contain your solutions. Read across the unshaded boxes to identify the answer to the quadrilateral question.

Tip: If an ordered pair *(a, b)* is a solution to a linear system, the point must satisfy both equations of the system. For example, (−1, 0) is a solution to the linear system $-x + y = 1$, $2x + y = -2$ because $-(-1) + 0 = 1$ and $2(-1) + 0 = -2$ are both true statements.

1. $5x - 2y = 14$ (−4, 2), (3, 1/2)
   $3x + 4y = 11$

2. $-5x + 3y = 25$ (0, −3), (−2, 5)
   $4x + 2y = 2$

3. $x + y = 5$ (−2, −4), (4, 1)
   $2x - y = 7$

4. $2x + 3y = 7$ (5, −1), (−5, 2)
   $x + y = 4$

5. $-4x + 3y = 10$ (2, −3), (−1, 2)
   $5x - 8y = -21$

6. $12x - 7y = 2$ (3/4, 1), (1, 1)
   $20x - 9y = 6$

7. $3x + y = 4$ (−9, 3), (−2, 10)
   $2x + y = 6$

8. $-3x + 5y = -2$ (−1, −1), (1, −1)
   $3x + 5y = -8$

9. $4x - y = 4$ (−3, 2), (1/4, −3)
   $4x + 2y = -5$

10. $4x + 3y = 14$ (3, 2), (2, 2)
    $9x - 2y = 14$

T	L	R	A	I
(−3, 2)	(4, 1)	(1, 1)	(−9, 3)	(3, 1/2)
P	U	E	O	Z
(0, −3)	(5, −1)	(−4, 2)	(1/4, −3)	(1, −1)
B	O	H	I	E
(−1, 2)	(−2, −4)	(3/4, 1)	(2, −3)	(2, 2)
D	M	Y	S	F
(3, 2)	(−1, −1)	(−2, 10)	(−5, 2)	(−2, 5)

Answer: _____

Name: _____   Date: _____   Class: _____

RECORD BREAKER

Who played in 3,562 baseball games and holds the record for the most games played in the world?

Solve each linear system given its graph. Check each answer algebraically. Below each set of equations, write the letter representing the matching solution. Read down each column of letters to identify the record-breaking athlete.

 Tip: The solution to a linear system is the point at which the two graphed lines intersect. Always confirm your answer algebraically by using the x and y values in both equations of the system. For example, if lines $3x + 2y = 4$ and $-x + 3y = -5$ intersect at point $(2, -1)$, then $3(2) + 2(-1) = 4$ and $-(2) + 3(-1) = -5$ should be true statements (which they are).

1. $8x - 3y = 15$
   $13x - 3y = 15$

   _____

2. $-3x + 5y = -2$
   $3x + 5y = -8$

   _____

3. $7x - 2y = 39$
   $5x + 2y = 21$

   _____

4. $x + y = 2$
   $x - 7y = -6$

   _____

5. $8x + 15y = 23$
   $7x + 10y = 17$

   _____

6. $4x - y = 8$
   $4x - 3y = 8$

   _____

7. $5x + 2y = 11$
   $7x + y = 10$

   _____

8. $-5x + 6y = 3$
   $x + y = 6$

   _____

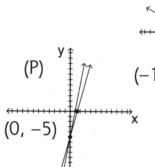
(P) (0, -5)

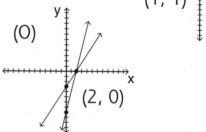
(E) (-1, -1)

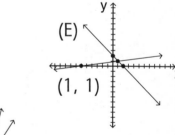
(E) (1, 1)

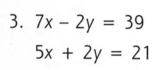
(O) (2, 0)

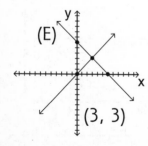
(E) (3, 3)

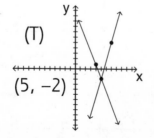
(T) (5, -2)

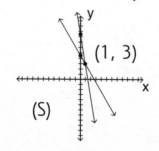
(1, 3) (S)

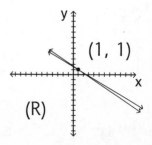
(1, 1) (R)

Date: _____ Class: _____

me: _____

HAMMIN' IT UP

What do they put on a criminal pig?

Solve the following linear systems by graphing. To reveal the riddle's answer at the bottom of the page, write the letter of each problem above its solution.

 Tip: To solve a linear system by graphing, you must graph both linear equations and find the point at which the two lines intersect. Always check the x and y values of your solution algebraically in both equations to confirm your answer.

M. $3x - 4y = -9$
  $-x - 4y = -13$

A. $-x + y = -2$
  $8x - 3y = -4$

C. $5x - 7y = 4$
  $-x + 8y = 19$

U. $y = -x$
  $y = x$

F. $5x - 2y = 14$
  $6x - 4y = 12$

S. $-9x - 10y = -11$
  $6x - 7y = -20$

H. $-2x + 6y = 8$
  $x = -1$

F. $3x - 5y = -14$
  $y = 4$

Answer:

___ ___ ___ ___ ___ ___ ___ ___
(–1,1) (–2,–4) (1,3) (5,3) (0,0) (4,3) (2,4) (–1,2)

Name: _____ Date: _____ Class: _____

MONSTROUS MAMMAL

What is the name of the largest mammal in the world—a creature that weighs up to 150 tons and measures up to 111.5-feet long?

Solve each linear system by using the substitution method. Find your solutions in the list of answers provided, and write the letters (in parenthesis) by the corresponding exercise numbers to spell out the two-word answer to the question.

 Tip: First, solve one equation in terms of y or x (for example, $3x + y = 2 \rightarrow y = 2 - 3x$). Second, substitute the expression into the other equation and solve for the remaining variable (for example, $x + 2y = 1 \rightarrow x + 2(2 - 3x) = 9 \rightarrow \mathbf{x = -1}$). Last, plug the value for the variable back into the first equation to solve for the first variable (for example, $3(-1) + y = 2 \rightarrow \mathbf{y = 5}$).

____ 1. $x + y = -4$ **and** $-x - 5y = -8$

____ 2. $2x + y = 3$ **and** $6x - y = 1$

____ 3. $-7x - y = -45$ **and** $4x - 2y = 0$

____ 4. $-3x + 6y = 24$ **and** $2x + y = -1$

____ 5. $-3x + y = 5$ **and** $2x - y = 5$

____ 6. $-x - y = -3$ **and** $x + 4y = 33$

____ 7. $8x - y = 10$ **and** $-2x - y = -20$

____ 8. $-3x + y = 11$ **and** $x + 5y = 39$

____ 9. $-2x - 2y = 0$ **and** $-x + y = -4$

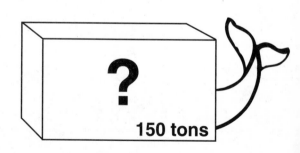

150 tons

(U) (5, 10)	(E) (−2, 3)	(W) (−10, −25)
(A) (3, 14)	(L) (−1, 8)	(E) (2, −2)
(B) (−7, 3)	(L) (1/2, 2)	(H) (−7, 10)

Date: Class:

MYTHICAL MATH

In Greek mythology, what was the name of the winged horse?

Solve each linear system by using the linear-combination method. Write each exercise number above its corresponding answer in the grid. To spell out the puzzler answer, write on each numbered line the code letter that corresponds to the given exercise number.

Tip: The following example shows how to solve linear systems through **linear combination.**

$$2x + y = -2 \qquad\qquad \rightarrow \quad 2x + y = -2$$
$$-x + y = 1 \rightarrow (2)(-x + y = 1) \rightarrow \underline{-2x + 2y = 2}$$
$$y = 0 \rightarrow \mathbf{y = 0};\ \text{and } 2x + (0) = -2 \rightarrow \mathbf{x = -1}$$

1. $-3x - 7y = 2$
   $x + 3y = -2$

2. $6x - y = -9$
   $-3x + 5y = 18$

3. $-7x + 8y = -2$
   $x + 3y = -8$

4. $-x + 11y = 3$
   $-x + y = -7$

5. $-5x - 4y = -22$
   $5x - 6y = -8$

6. $-x - y = -2$
   $4x + 7y = 11$

7. $-7x + 9y = 3$
   $6x - 4y = 16$

8. $2x - 3y = -11$
   $-3x + 4y = 16$

Code Letter	A	E	G	I	N	P	S	U
Exercise #								
Answer	(−4, 1)	(8, 1)	(4, −2)	(1, 1)	(6, 5)	(−2, −2)	(2, 3)	(−1, 3)

Answer:

___ ___ ___ ___ ___ ___ ___
3   4   1   8   5   2   5

ood Apple GA1687

BATTER UP

What do catchers eat off of for dinner?

On a separate piece of paper, graph each linear system. From the pair of answers provided, select the one that describes the graph and circle the corresponding letter. Read the circled letters downward to identify the two-word answer to the catchy riddle.

 Tip: A linear system has many solutions if the two equations graph as the same line. If the equations graph as parallel lines, the linear system has no solution.

1. $-2x - 3y = 6$
   $4x + 6y = -12$
       (H) Has many solutions   (D) Has no solution

2. $-x + y = -7$
   $-x + y = 1$
       (I) Has many solutions   (O) Has no solution

3. $-6x - 3y = 15$
   $y = -2x - 5$
       (N) Has no solution   (M) Has many solutions

4. $4x + 2y = -5$
   $4x + 2y = -6$
       (E) Has no solution   (N) Has many solutions

5. $-2x + 6y = -6$
   $-6x + 18y = -18$
       (E) Has no solution   (P) Has many solutions

6. $-10x + 5y = 20$
   $y = 2x + 5$
       (L) Has no solution   (R) Has many solutions

7. $5x - 10y = -90$
   $-5x + 10y = 30$
       (W) Has many solutions   (A) Has no solution

8. $x = -4$
   $x = 2$
       (T) Has no solution   (A) Has many solutions

9. $y = -2x - 6$
   $4x - 2y = 5$
       (R) Has many solutions   (E) Has no solution

Answer: _____

Name: Date: Class:

TASTY TREAT

The largest one ever made weighed 3,011 pounds and was peppermint-flavored. What was it?

Graph each system of linear inequalities. In front of each exercise number, write the letter representing the quadrants where the solution can be found. Read down the column of letters to identify the answer to the trivia teaser.

Tip: On one grid, graph each equation of the system. Then identify the part of the grid in which the shaded areas of the individual graphs overlap. Remember that the solution to a linear system of inequalities is a shaded region, not just a single point.

Column A

_____ 1. $x - 2y \geq 3$

         $x - 2y \geq -5$

_____ 2. $x \geq 2$

         $y \leq 4$

_____ 3. $3x + 2y \leq 6$

         $x \geq 3$

_____ 4. $3x - 4y \leq 12$

         $-2x + 5y \geq 10$

_____ 5. $x < 5, \; y < 3$

         $x + y \leq 4$

_____ 6. $x < -2, \; y > -5$

         $-2x - y > 3$

_____ 7. $x + y < 6$

         $x > 3, \; y > 0$

_____ 8. $x \leq -1, \; x \geq -5$

         $y \leq 0, \; y \geq -3$

Column B

P. Quadrants II and III

L. Quadrants I, II, and III

O. Quadrant I

L. Quadrants I, III, and IV

I. Quadrants I, II, III, and IV

O. Quadrants I and IV

P. Quadrant III

L. Quadrant IV

Reproducible

ood Apple GA1687

Name: Date: Class:

REVIEW WHAT YOU KNOW
ABOUT SOLVING LINEAR SYSTEMS

Circle the ordered pair that is the solution to the linear system.

1. $2x + 3y = 4$ $(3, 4), (-1, 2)$

    $3x - y = -5$

3. $x - y = 2$ $(2, 0), (-2, 0)$

    $2x + y = 4$

2. $4x + y = 5$ $(1/2, 3), (2, -3)$

    $-4x + 2y = 4$

4. $4x + 3y = 24$ $(-4, 3), (3, 4)$

    $2x - y = 2$

Solve the following linear systems by graphing.

5. $y = x + 1$

    $y = -x + 3$

6. $3x - 4y = 5$

    $x = 3$

Solve the following linear systems by using substitution.

7. $y = x - 3$

    $4x + y = 32$

8. $2x + y = 1$

    $x - y = 2$

Solve the following linear systems using linear combinations.

9. $2x + 5y = 9$

    $3x - 5y = 1$

10. $3x - y = 13$

     $5x + 2y = 7$

Graph the following systems and describe their solution(s).

11. $x + y = -1$

     $x + y = 8$

12. $-6x + 4y = -6$

     $3x - 2y = 3$

Graph each linear inequality system.

13. $x + y \le 5$

     $x \ge 2$

     $y \ge 0$

14. $x + y \le 10$

     $2x + y \ge 10$

     $x - y \le 2$

me: Date: Class:

BELIEVE IT OR NOT

In 1987, in the country of Australia, 46 people piled onto one of these vehicles and rode on it for one mile. What were they riding?

Simplify the problems. Find each answer in the list provided, and circle the corresponding letter. Unscramble the circled letters to discover the answer to the amazing fact.

Tip: When solving multiplication problems involving exponents, remember $a^m \cdot a^n = a^{m+n}$, $(a^m)^n = a^m \cdot {}^n$, and $(ab)^m = a^m \cdot b^m$. Don't forget to apply the exponents to both parts of a variable term. For example,
$3x^2(2x^2)^3 \rightarrow 3x^2(2^3x^6) \rightarrow 3x^2 \cdot 8x^6 \rightarrow 24x^{2+6} \rightarrow 24x^8$.

1. $3^2 \cdot 3^4$

2. $(x^3)^5$

3. $(-4x^2)^3$

4. $x \cdot x^7$

5. $(4 \cdot 3)^2$

6. $7x^3(2x^4)^3$

7. $(-6x)^2$

8. $(3x)^4 \cdot x$

9. $[(7 + x)^4]^3$

10. $(2x^2)^3(-x^4)$

(U)	(Y)	(M)	(O)	(C)	(E)
3^8	x^{15}	x^8	$56x^{15}$	$-8x^{10}$	$36x^2$
(T)	(C)	(I)	(N)	(G)	(B)
144	$81x^5$	$-8x^3$	$-9x^8$	$(7 + x)^7$	$3x^4$
(W)	(S)	(H)	(R)	(O)	(L)
$3x^{10}$	$64x^4$	-24^{10}	$(7 + x)^{12}$	$-64x^6$	3^6

Answer: _____

th...

Name: Date: Class:

SHAPING UP

What's a polygon with 5 sides? What's a quadrilateral with sides of equal length? What's a quadrilateral with opposite sides that are parallel and of equal length?

Simplify each problem. Write the exercise number in front of the corresponding answer listed in the grid. To spell out the answers at the bottom of the page, refer to the grid and write the code letter that corresponds to the exercise number given.

 Tip: Rearrange the variables at the final stages of simplification (no parenthesis) so that like-variables are next to each other. For example, $x^2y^4x^3yz \rightarrow x^2x^3y^4yz \rightarrow x^5y^5z$. Note that exponents of different variables cannot be added together.

1. $(x^2 \cdot x^3)^3$

2. $(2x)^2$

3. $(-8x^3)^2 \cdot x^3$

4. $(-xy)^2(x^2y^4)$

5. $(2x)^3 \cdot (2x^3)^3$

6. $(-2x)(3xy)(4y)$

7. $(3x)(3x^2)$

8. $(x^2y)(2xy^2)(4xy)$

9. $(xy^2)(x^2y)^2$

10. $(-4x^2)^3$

11. $(-x^3)(4x^3)^2$

12. $(-5xy)^2(x^2y^2)$

13. $(2x^4)^3$

14. $(-3xy^3)^2(-2x)^3$

15. $(5x)^2 \cdot x^3$

16. $(3x^2yz^2)^3(xyz)$

17. $(-x^4)(9x^3)^2$

18. $(-x^3yz)^4(-3z^5)^3$

Code Letter	Exercise #	Answer
A		$-64x^6$
B		$-27x^{12}y^4z^{19}$
C		$64x^9$
D		x^5y^4
E		$-72x^5y^6$
G		$64x^{12}$
H		$-16x^9$
I		$-24x^2y^2$
L		x^{15}
M		$27x^7y^4z^7$
N		x^4y^6
O		$8x^4y^4$
P		$8x^{12}$
Q		$-81x^{10}$
R		$4x^2$
S		$9x^3$
T		$25x^4y^4$
U		$25x^5$

Answer:

13	14	4	12	10	5	8	4		2	11	8	16	18	15	7

13	10	2	10	1	1	14	1	8	5	2	10	16

Name: _____ Date: _____ Class: _____

PRESIDENTIAL STATE

This state, known for its many dams, generates more power from water than any other state. It is also the only state named for a president. What state is it?

Use the values $x = 1$ and $y = 2$ to simplify each exponential term. Solve the problems in numerical order and find your answers in the list provided. Write the corresponding letters on the "answer line" to reveal the name of the state.

 Tip: When taking the power of a negative number, the negative sign is included in the calculation, unless it is outside a parenthesis.
For example, $(-3)^2 = -3 \bullet -3 \rightarrow 9$, and $-(3)^2 = -(3 \bullet 3) \rightarrow -9$.

1. $(x^3y^2)^2$

2. $-2x^3y$

3. $-xy^3$

4. $y^3 \bullet y^2$

5. $(x^3 \bullet y)^3$

6. $(x^5y^3)^2$

7. $(y^3 \bullet y^2)(-2x^3)^2$

8. $(x^6y^2)^3(xy)^2$

9. $[(y^3 + x^5)]^2$

10. $[(y^2 \bullet y^3 + xy^2)] + (x^3y^2)^2$

(S) -8 (M) -6 (I) 8 (N) 52 (H) 14

(N) 64 (E) -16 (A) -4 (T) 256 (B) 36

(O) 81 (K) -18 (G) 128 (H) 32 (W) 16

Answer: _____

ood Apple GA1687

Name: _____   Date: _____   Class: _____

ANCIENT CALCULATOR

Long before calculators were invented, this mathematical tool was used to quickly add numbers. A skilled individual can use this device to add up to fifteen numbers in one minute. What is the tool called?

Simplify the exponential terms. Match your answers to those given. Write in front of each exercise number the letter representing the solution. Use the letters from the odd-numbered problems to spell out the answer to the question.

 Tip: Remember that $a^{-n} = 1/a^n$ and $1/a^{-n} = a^n$ and $a^0 = 1$ (when a $\uparrow$ 0). Keep in mind that a number in front of a variable with a negative exponent is not inverted. For example, $5x^{-8}y^{-3} = 5/(x^8y^3)$.

____ 1. x^{-5} (U) y^2

____ 2. $x^{-3}y^4$ (B) y^3/x^6

____ 3. x^{-6}/y^{-3} (C) 1

____ 4. $1/(x^{-2}y^{-3})$ (N) $-4/y^5$

____ 5. $x^{-1}y$ (U) x^2y^3

____ 6. $(-4x)^0y^{-3}$ (A) $1/x^5$

____ 7. x^0y^0 (K) $1/(25x^2)$

____ 8. $(4x)^{-1}(3y^{-2})$ (T) $1/y^3$

____ 9. $1/(x^0y^{-2})$ (P) y^4/x^3

____ 10. $(-5x)^{-2}$ (A) y/x

____ 11. $3/(x^{-4}y^3)$ (S) $3x^4/y^3$

____ 12. $(-4x^0)(y^{-5})$ (C) $3/(4xy^2)$

Answer: _____

Name: _____   Date: _____   Class: _____

IN THE BLINK OF AN EYE

How many times do most people blink their eyes in one minute?

Simplify each term. Shade in the grid boxes that contain your solutions. Read across the remaining unshaded boxes to spell out the two-word answer to the question.

Tip: To divide powers that have the same base, remember that $a^m/a^n = a^{m-n}$. To determine the power of a quotient or a fraction in parenthesis, distribute the power to both the numerator and the denominator: $(a/b)^m = a^m/b^m$, where $b \uparrow 0$.
For example $(-3/4)^3 \rightarrow (-3)^3/4^3 \rightarrow -27/64$.

1. $5^3/5^2$

2. $(2/3)^3$

3. $(-1/4)^2$

4. $(5/6)^{-1}$

5. $(-9)^{-2}/9^{-1}$

6. $2^3/2^{-2}$

7. $(-1/5)^{-3}$

8. $(5 \cdot 5^4)/5^3$

9. $(-3)^2/3^2$

10. $-6^5/6^5$

11. $2^2/2^{-2}$

12. $7^8/7^5$

13. $3^5/3^2$

14. $(-4/7)^{-2}$

15. $8^{-3}/8^{-1}$

16. $(9^{-3} \cdot 9^{-4})/9^{-8}$

A	F	U	I	O	H	P
1/9	−147	49/16	−3	5	25	16
F	B	R	T	Q	E	M
6	1	8/27	−32	9	14	343
E	C	N	Y	A	T	K
0	−125	15	1/16	1/64	8	27
I	D	M	L	E	R	S
6/7	6/5	−4	−1	7	32	21

Answer: _____

Name: Date: Class:

PLASTIC PROBLEMS

The sturdiness of plastic makes it good for many things, but not for the environment. How many years can it take for a plastic bottle to rot away?

Simplify each expression so that all exponents are positive values. Place the final exponent (power) of each answer in the appropriate position in the cross-number puzzle. Read across the rows to identify the highlighted boxes, and write the corresponding numbers in sequence to reveal the answer to the question.

 Tip: Remember that $(1/a^n)^{-m} = (a^n)^m$ and $(a^n)^{-m} = (1/a^n)^m$.
For example, $(1/3^2)^{-2} \rightarrow (3^2)^2 \rightarrow (9)^2 \rightarrow 81$.

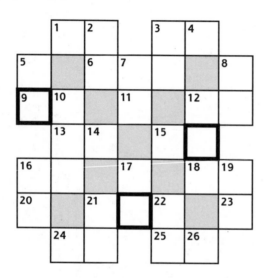

Across

1. x^{33}/x^{10}
3. y^{-3}/y^{-32}
5. y^3/y
6. x^{90}/x^{-20}
8. y^{-4}/y^{-5}
9. x^{50}/x^9
11. y^{21}/y^{14}
12. y^{100}/y^{84}
13. x^{25}/x^6

15. $(1/x^5)^{-6}$
16. y^{35}/y^7
17. y^{-4}/y^{-8}
18. $(1/x^{-17})^3$
20. x^{-2}/x^{-8}
21. x^{110}/x^7
23. $(1/y^{-1})^8$
24. $(1/x^{17})^{-2}$
25. x^{-32}/x^{-59}

Down

1. y^{-3}/y^{-5}
2. x^{13}/x^{-18}
3. x^{100}/x^{80}
4. $(1/y^{-1})^9$
5. y^{36}/y^{12}
7. x^{13}/x^{-4}
8. x^{12}/x^{-4}
10. y^{120}/y^2
12. x^{100}/x^{-5}

14. $(1/y^{-3})^3$
15. $(x^3/x^2)^3$
16. x^{13}/x^{-13}
17. $(x^2)^5/x^{-30}$
19. $(1/y^3)^{-6}$
21. y^{-52}/y^{-66}
22. x^{52}/x^{20}
26. x^{10}/x^3

Name: Date: Class:

EXPONENT ASSIGNMENT

What do you get when you add one homework assignment and one homework assignment?

Simplify each exponential term. At the bottom of the page, write the letter of each problem above its solution to spell out the answer to the riddle.

 Tip: To simplify a term raised to a negative power, change the value to its reciprocal and raise it to the positive power. For example, $16 \cdot 2^{-3} \rightarrow (16)(1/2^3) \rightarrow (16)(1/8) \rightarrow 2$.

M. $1/6^{-2}$

U. $4^{-2} \cdot 4^2$

O. $-3^0 \cdot 1/3^{-2}$

K. 4^{-2}

T. $-(5^{-1})^{-2}$

H. $-2 \cdot (-2)^{-2}$

R. $-(4 \cdot 3)^0$

C. $1/(9x^0)^{-1}$

O. $(-10)^0/(-10)^2$

W. $-(8^{-5} \cdot 8^5) \cdot 3$

H. $7^4 \cdot 7^{-3}$

W. $(-3)^{-9} \cdot (-3)^{10}$

E. $6 \cdot 6^{-1} \cdot 5$

M. $2^5 \cdot 2^{-3}$

O. $11^9 \cdot 11^{-7}$

Answer:

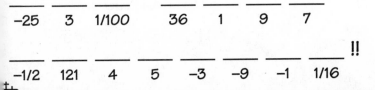

___	___	___	___	___	___	___
−25	3	1/100	36	1	9	7

___	___	___	___	___	___	___	!!
−1/2	121	4	5	−3	−9	−1	1/16

Name: _____   Date: _____   Class: _____

WHIGGISH REPUBLICAN

He served in the Illinois legislature as a Whig before becoming the first republican president of the United States. Who was this well-known man?

Change problems 1–7 from scientific notation to decimal form, and change problems 8–14 from decimal form to scientific notation. Match your answers to those given. Write in front of each exercise number the letter representing the solution. Read down the columns of letters to reveal the two-word answer to the question.

 Tip: To change a number from scientific notation ($a \times 10^n$) to standard decimal form, move the decimal in the a term to the right when n is positive and to the left when n is negative. To change a number from standard decimal form to scientific notation, reverse the process. For example, $3.45 \times 10^2 \rightarrow 345$; and $0.0345 \rightarrow 3.45 \times 10^{-2}$.

_____ 1. 1.3456×10^5

_____ 2. 4.5×10^3

_____ 3. 7.803×10^{-2}

_____ 4. 8.39×10^{-5}

_____ 5. 5.23×10^7

_____ 6. 1.3×10^{-4}

_____ 7. 7.51×10^{-1}

_____ 8. 0.000751

_____ 9. 0.00751

_____ 10. $75,100$

_____ 11. $751,000,000$

_____ 12. $7,510$

_____ 13. 0.000000751

_____ 14. 75.1

(M) 13,000

(H) 52,300,000

(A) 0.0000839

(N) 7.51×10

(N) 7.51×10^4

(A) 0.00013

(M) 0.751

(J) 0.000456

(B) 4,500

(C) 2,920

(H) 0.00007023

(R) 0.07803

(I) 7.51×10^{-3}

(C) 7.51×10^8

(L) 7.51×10^{-7}

(S) 374,500

(L) 7.51×10^{-4}

(O) 7.51×10^3

(I) 0.00292

(G) 0.00009524

(N) 0.0000003275

(L) 45,600

(A) 134,560

(F) 0.000000086

Name: Date: Class:

AWARD-WINNING MATH

In 1995, which Tom Hanks film received thirteen Oscar nominations, including Best Actor and Best Picture?

Solve each problem, and round the answer to the nearest hundredth. Circle the letter that is next to the matching solution. Read down the list of circled answers to identify the name of the talented actor.

 Tip: When multiplying or dividing numbers written in scientific notation, treat the 10^n term as if it was a variable—do not multiply out the exponent. Remember: Final answers should have only one digit to the left of the decimal.
For example, $(8.4 \times 10^5) / (4.2 \times 10^3) \rightarrow (8.4/4.2)(10^5/10^3) \rightarrow 2.0 \times 10^2$.

1. $(6 \times 10^8)(6 \times 10^{-2})$ (F) 3.6×10^7 (D) 2.95×10^{-4}

2. $\dfrac{6.5 \times 10^3}{4.2 \times 10^{-4}}$ (O) 1.55×10^7 (C) 4×10^{-7}

3. $\dfrac{5.4 \times 10^{-2}}{3.4 \times 10^{-3}}$ (H) 9.23×10^{-3} (R) 1.59×10

4. $(5 \times 10^4)(4.2 \times 10^{-2})$ (R) 2.1×10^3 (A) 9.39×10^4

5. $(1.4 \times 10^3)(3.2 \times 10^4)$ (A) 4.56×10^4 (E) 4.48×10^7

6. $(2.5 \times 10^{-5})(9.1 \times 10^9)$ (K) 1.97×10^9 (S) 2.28×10^5

7. $\dfrac{7.6 \times 10^{-4}}{4.3 \times 10^{-6}}$ (I) 2.59×10^{-8} (T) 1.77×10^2

8. $(7.8 \times 10^5)(4.4 \times 10^{-7})$ (G) 3.43×10^{-1} (B) 8.4×10^{-2}

9. $\dfrac{8.4 \times 10^{-7}}{2.34 \times 10^{-6}}$ (U) 3.59×10^{-1} (W) 5.32×10^8

10. $\dfrac{1.2 \times 10^7}{5.5 \times 10^4}$ (N) 7.5×10^2 (M) 2.18×10^2

11. $(9.8 \times 10^{-2})(1.5 \times 10^{-5})$ (P) 1.47×10^{-6} (Y) 7.52×10^{-5}

Name: Date: Class:

REVIEW WHAT YOU KNOW
ABOUT WORKING WITH EXPONENTS

Simplify each exponential term.

1. 3^{-2}

2. $5^3 \cdot 5^{-1}$

3. $9^4 \cdot 9^{-4}$

4. $4 \cdot 4^{-1}$

5. $3^0 \cdot 4^{-2}$

6. $(5^2 \cdot 5)/5^2$

7. $(2x)^3 \, (-x^2)$

8. $(-a^3) \, / \, (4a^2)^2$

9. $(3x^2y^2/3xy)(6xy^3/3y)$

10. $(4xy^3/2y)(5xy^{-3}/x^2)$

Change each expression from scientific notation to decimal form.

11. 2.54×10^{-3}

12. 3.1×10^4

13. 7.25×10^{-2}

14. 9.26×10^7

15. 4.3×10^{-8}

Change each expression from decimal form to scientific notation.

16. 0.00000096

17. 123,000,000

18. 0.00041

19. 8,400,000

20. 0.0000087

me: _____ Date: _____ Class: _____

DECLARING INDEPENDENCE

Which U.S. state was the first colony to set up its own government, six months before the Declaration of Independence was signed?

Solve each problem and round decimal answers to the nearest hundredth. Shade in the grid boxes that contain your solutions. Read across the unshaded boxes to identify the answer to the history question.

 Tip: The square root is the reverse of a square ($\sqrt{b^2} = b$). When taking the square root of a number, look to see if the value is a **perfect square**—a whole number that has been squared. For example, *121* is a perfect square because $\sqrt{121} \rightarrow \sqrt{(11)^2} \rightarrow 11$.

1. $\sqrt{64}$
2. $-\sqrt{49}$
3. $\sqrt{0}$
4. $-\sqrt{1}$
5. $\sqrt{-25}$
6. $\sqrt{81}$
7. $-\sqrt{144}$
8. $\sqrt{0.16}$
9. $\sqrt{625}$
10. $-\sqrt{256}$

11. $\sqrt{52}$
12. $-\sqrt{100}$
13. $-\sqrt{121}$
14. $\sqrt{36}$
15. $\sqrt{(9/4)}$
16. $-\sqrt{(49/36)}$
17. $\sqrt{(25/169)}$
18. $-\sqrt{(1/64)}$
19. $-\sqrt{11}$
20. $\sqrt{0.25}$

D 0.4	N −5	P 6	U −7/6	E 22	Y −7	R −12	W 20
F −3.32	Q −1	H −3	S 7.21	A −13	J 9	M 14	P 15
S 12	L 3/2	V −1/8	H 21	I 8.13	W −10	N 8	T 25
G 5/13	V 0	R 17	U undefined	O −16	E −18	P 0.5	F −11

Answer: _____

ood Apple GA1687

Name: _____ Date: _____ Class: _____

MOON WALK

Which American astronaut became the first person to walk on the moon?

Solve for x. Find your solutions in the list of answers given. Write in front of each exercise number the letter representing its solution to spell out the name of the famous space explorer.

 Tip: To solve for x in the equation $x^2 = d$, where d is an integer, take the square root of both sides of the equation. Remember there are always two solutions when d is positive ($\sqrt{x^2} = \sqrt{d} \rightarrow x = \pm d$), but no solution when d is negative ($\sqrt{x^2} = \sqrt{-d} \rightarrow$ no solution). For example, $2x^2 = 162 \rightarrow x^2 = 81 \rightarrow \sqrt{x^2} = \sqrt{81} \rightarrow x = \pm 9$.

_____ 1. $x^2 = 16$

_____ 2. $x^2 = 49$

_____ 3. $x^2 = 100$

_____ 4. $4x^2 = 100$

_____ 5. $6x^2 = 0$

_____ 6. $3x^2 = 192$

_____ 7. $10x^2 - 15 = 2235$

_____ 8. $2x^2 + 5 = 3$

_____ 9. $x^2 + 15 = 24$

_____ 10. $7x^2 + 9 = 16$

_____ 11. $9x^2 + 28 = 29$

_____ 12. $x^2 - 23 = 13$

_____ 13. $4x^2 + 4 = 5$

(R) ± 1	(N) ± 4	(E) ± 7	(A) 0
(L) ± 5	(I) ± 10	(O) $\pm 1/3$	(G) $\pm 1/2$
(S) no solution	(T) ± 3	(N) ± 6	(R) ± 8
(M) ± 15			

Answer: _____

Name: Date: Class:

TOOLIN' THROUGH MATH

What tool do you need in math?

For each exercise, use the Pythagorean formula to solve for the missing value. (Round decimals to the nearest hundredth.) Draw a line from each set of values in Column A to its matching solution in Column B. Write in front of the exercise number the corresponding letter. Read down the column of written letters to reveal the answer to the riddle.

 Tip: For any right triangle with hypotenuse c and sides a and b, remember that $a^2 + b^2 = c^2$ (the Pythagorean formula), and $c = \sqrt{(a^2 + b^2)}$.

    For example, if $a = 2$ and $b = 3$, then $c = \sqrt{(2^2 + 3^2)} \rightarrow \sqrt{(4 + 9)} \rightarrow \sqrt{13} \rightarrow 3.61$.

Column A

____ 1. $a = 4, b = 6, c = ?$

____ 2. $a = 7, b = 9, c = ?$

____ 3. $a = 3, b = 8, c = ?$

____ 4. $b = 14, c = 20, a = ?$

____ 5. $b = 9, c = 29, a = ?$

____ 6. $b = 13, c = 39, a = ?$

____ 7. $b = 21, c = 41, a = ?$

____ 8. $a = 3, c = 7, b = ?$

____ 9. $a = 6, c = 12, b = ?$

____ 10. $a = 18, c = 25, b = ?$

____ 11. $a = 30, c = 40, b = ?$

Column B

(P)   36.77

(S)   26.46

(I)   27.57

(M)   7.21

(E)   10.39

(L)   8.54

(T)   14.28

(R)   17.35

(U)   11.40

(I)   6.32

(L)   35.21

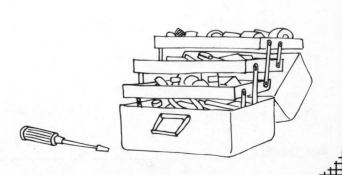

Name: Date: Class:

QUAZY QUADRATIC

It's not just a picture, but a puzzle! Can you identify the meaning of the wacky-word illustration?

Determine the solutions to each quadratic equation. As you solve the problems in numerical order, draw a line connecting the labeled golf holes that match your solutions. The letters of the corresponding flags will spell out the four-word answer to the "quazy" puzzle.

 Tip: The solutions to the quadratic equation $ax^2 + bx + c = 0$ can be found by plugging the values of a, b, and c into the quadratic formula $x = \dfrac{-b \pm \sqrt{b^2 - 4ac}}{2a}$.

1. $x^2 + 15x + 54 = 0$

2. $3x^2 + 6x - 24 = 0$

3. $x^2 + 7x + 10 = 0$

4. $2x^2 + 2x - 40 = 0$

5. $3x^2 - 22x + 7 = 0$

6. $3x^2 - 2x - 16 = 0$

7. $5x^2 - 6x - 8 = 0$

8. $7x^2 + 9x - 10 = 0$

9. $-x^2 - 3x - 2 = 0$

10. $4x^2 - 10x + 4 = 0$

N $x = -6, -9$

T $x = -5, -2$

2	**par**
t	
o	
n	

P $x = 5/7, -2$

U $x = 4, -5$

P $x = 7, 1/3$

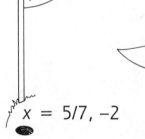

T $x = 8/3, -2$

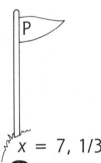

O

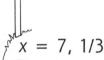

O $x = 2, -4$

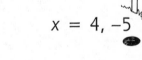

R $x = 1/2, 2$

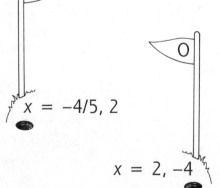

A $x = -4/5, 2$

$x = -1, -2$

Answer: _____

Name: Date: Class:

HOME RUN

Reggie Jackson and Babe Ruth share the world-record title for the most home runs hit in a single game. How many home runs did they hit?

Calculate the discriminant of each quadratic, and then use your results to determine the number of solutions for each equation. Count the number of quadratics that have no solution—your total will equal the answer to the baseball stumper.

 Tip: When solving a quadratic equation, the *discriminant* $(b^2 - 4ac)$ indicates how many solutions there are. If $b^2 - 4ac$ is positive, the equation has two solutions; if $b^2 - 4ac$ is zero, the equation has one solution; and if $b^2 - 4ac$ is negative, the equation has no solution.

Quadratic Equations	Discriminant $(b^2 - 4ac)$	Number of Solutions
1. $x^2 + 2x - 3 = 0$		
2. $-x^2 - 4x - 12 = 0$		
3. $x^2 - 4x + 4 = 0$		
4. $7x^2 + 3x + 2 = 0$		
5. $-2x^2 - 2x + 5 = 0$		
6. $5x^2 - 6x + 2 = 0$		
7. $3x^2 - 6x + 3 = 0$		
8. $-x^2 - x + 5 = 0$		
9. $x^2 + 7x + 12 = 0$		
10. $x^2 - 2x + 1 = 0$		

Answer: _____

Name: _____   Date: _____   Class: _____

PERPLEXING PARABOLAS

Every four years, a different city from around the world hosts the summer Olympic Games. Los Angeles was the site of the summer Olympic Games in the year 198___ .

Determine the vertex for each quadratic equation. State whether the corresponding graph (a parabola) opens up or opens down. Count the number of graphs that open up—your total will equal the missing number in the trivia statement.

 Tip: Every quadratic equation $ax^2 + bx + c = 0$ graphs as a *parabola*—a *U*-shaped curve. When the value of a is positive, the parabola opens up; when a is negative, the parabola opens down. The vertex (x, y) of the parabola can by determined by using the equation $x = -b/2a$, and then plugging the x value into the equation to solve for y.

1. $y = -7x^2 + 14x + 2$

2. $y = 5x^2 + 20x - 3$

3. $y = -x^2 + x + 5$

4. $y = x^2$

5. $y = -x^2 - 10$

6. $y = -x^2 - 2x - 6$

7. $y = -3x^2 + 12x - 8$

8. $y = x^2 + 8x - 1$

9. $y = -4x^2 - 16x + 3$

10. $y = x^2 + 8x + 20$

Answer: _____

Name: _____ Date: _____ Class: _____

MANY MULTIPLES

Mrs. Feodor Vassilyev of Shuya, Russia, holds the world record for having the most sets of quadruplets. How many sets did she have?

On a separate piece of paper, draw the graph (parabola) of each quadratic equation. Count the number of parabolas that open up—your total will equal the answer to the trivia question.

 Tip: When plotting a graph of a quadratic equation, first calculate and plot the vertex. Then set up a "table of values" that includes x values greater than and less than the x-coordinate of the vertex. Plug each x value into the equation to solve for the corresponding y.

1. $y = -2x^2 + 8x - 4$

2. $y = x^2 + 4x + 3$

3. $y = -x^2$

4. $y = -x^2 - 6$

5. $y = -3x^2 - 18x - 25$

6. $y = -x^2 + 2x - 1$

7. $y = x^2 + 5$

8. $y = 4x^2 + 16x + 20$

9. $y = -5x^2 - 20x - 19$

10. $y = x^2 + 6x + 4$

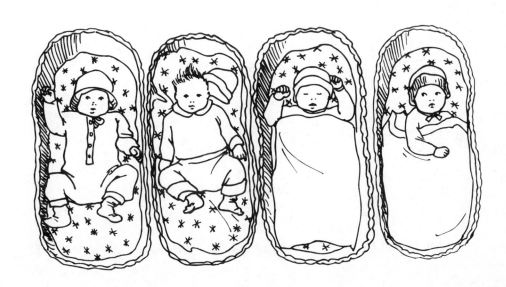

Answer: _____

ood Apple GA1687

REVIEW WHAT YOU KNOW ABOUT SQUARE ROOTS AND QUADRATIC EQUATIONS

Solve the following equations for x.

1. $x^2 = 16$

2. $-2x^2 = -50$

3. $4x^2 + 7 = 8$

4. $1/2x^2 - 1 = 7$

5. $-3x^2 = -363$

Use the Pythagorean formula to solve for a, b, or c in the following problems. Round your answers to the nearest hundredth.

6. $a = 4$, $b = 3$, $c = ?$

7. $a = 6$, $c = 10$, $b = ?$

8. $b = 13$, $c = 15$, $a = ?$

9. $a = 9$, $b = 12$, $c = ?$

10. $b = 28$, $c = 35$, $a = ?$

Use the quadratic formula to solve the following equations.

11. $5x^2 - 6x - 8 = 0$

12. $-x^2 - 3x - 2 = 0$

13. $3x^2 - 22x + 7 = 0$

14. $2x^2 + 2x - 40 = 0$

15. $4x^2 - 10x + 4 = 0$

Sketch the graphs of the following quadratic equations. Label the vertex of each graph.

16. $y = x^2 + 6x + 5$

17. $y = -x^2 - 2x - 3$

me: Date: Class:

SECRET SHAPE

How well *do you know your shapes*? See if you can identify the secret shape from the clue words you decode.

Add the following polynomials. Write the exercise number in front of the corresponding answer listed in the grid. To spell out the words at the bottom of the page, refer to the grid and write the code letter that corresponds to the exercise number given.

Tip: When combining two polynomials, add the coefficients of like terms. For example,
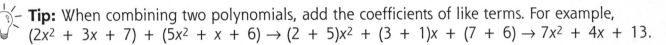
$(2x^2 + 3x + 7) + (5x^2 + x + 6) \rightarrow (2 + 5)x^2 + (3 + 1)x + (7 + 6) \rightarrow 7x^2 + 4x + 13.$

1. $(x^2 + 2x + 4) + (3x^2 + 2x + 5)$
2. $(3x^2 - 2x + 7) + (5x^2 + 8x - 5)$
3. $(x^2 - 7x + 4) + (9x^2 + 6x + 4)$
4. $(2x^2 + 7) + (-7x^2 - 8)$
5. $(-6x^2 + 5x - 3) + (x^2 - 2x + 7)$
6. $(-3x^2 + 4) + (-9x^2 - 5x + 3)$
7. $(5x^2 - 10x + 3) + (4x^2 - 1)$
8. $(x^2 + 2x - 1) + (x^3 - 2x + 1)$
9. $(3x^3 - 4x^2) + (7x^2 + 6)$
10. $(-12x^2 - x + 8) + (9x^2 - 16)$
11. $(-x^2 - x - 1) + (-x^2 - 3x + 7)$
12. $(13x^3 - 6x - 15) + (-9x^2 + 15)$
13. $(-4x^2 - 3x - 9) + (8x^2 + 5x + 10)$
14. $(-10x^2 + 14) + (x^3 + 9x^2)$
15. $(-8x^2 + 2x - 6) + (x + 4)$
16. $(2x^3 - 2x^2 - 10) + (3x^3 + 5)$

Code Letter	Exercise #	Answer
A		$8x^2 + 6x + 2$
C		$3x^3 + 3x^2 + 6$
D		$x^3 - x^2 + 14$
E		$-5x^2 + 3x + 4$
F		$x^3 + x^2$
G		$13x^3 - 9x^2 - 6x$
H		$4x^2 + 4x + 9$
I		$5x^3 - 2x^2 - 5$
M		$-3x^2 - x - 8$
N		$10x^2 - x + 8$
O		$9x^2 - 10x + 2$
P		$-5x^2 - 1$
R		$4x^2 + 2x + 1$
S		$-8x^2 + 3x - 2$
T		$-2x^2 - 4x + 6$
U		$-12x^2 - 5x + 7$

Answer:

___ ___ ___ ___ ___
9   1   7   13   14

___ ___ ___ ___ ___ ___   ___ ___ ___ ___ ___ ___
15   5   9   11   7   13   13   2   14   16   6   15

___ ___ ___ ___ ___ ___ ___ ___ ___ ___ ___ ___
9   16   13   9   6   10   8   5   13   5   3   9   5

The words describe which shape? _____

m...

ood Apple GA1687

Name: _____   Date: _____   Class: _____

PUZZLING PROBLEM

It may look like a math equation, but the problem written on the chalkboard is truly puzzling. Can you figure out the wacky-word solution?

Solve each problem. From the list of answers provided, circle the letters that are next to the matching solutions. Write the letters in front of their corresponding exercise numbers to spell out the two-word answer to the puzzler.

 Tip: When subtracting one polynomial from another, group together and subtract like terms. For example,
$(12x^2 + 3x + 7) - (5x^2 + x - 12) \rightarrow (12 - 5)x^2 + (3 - 1)x + 7 - (-12) \rightarrow 7x^2 + 2x + 19.$

____ 1. $(-x^2 - 2x - 3) - (-x^2 - 3x - 4)$

____ 2. $(x + 10) - (x^2 - 10x + 9)$

____ 3. $(-3x^3 - 2x^2 + 7x - 2) - (8x^3 - 2)$ (N) $9x^2 - 4x + 1$

____ 4. $(4x^2 + 9x + 5) - (2x^2 + 6x + 3)$ (T) $-11x^3 - 2x^2 + 7x$

____ 5. $(-2x^2 - 8) - (x^2 + 2x + 9)$ (D) $-3x^3 - 2x^2 + 6x - 1$

____ 6. $(6x^3 + 3) - (5x^3 + 2x^2 - 2)$ (S) $-3x^2 - 6x + 4$

____ 7. $(10x^3 - 15) - (15x^3 + 5x - 11)$ (T) $x + 1$

____ 8. $(2x^2 - 8x + 3) - (5x^2 - 2x - 1)$ (B) $7x^2 - 4x$

____ 9. $(x^3 - 4x + 1) - (x^2 - 2x + 5)$ (A) $2x^2 + 3x + 2$

(O) $-x^2 + 11x + 1$

(F) $-x^3 + 3x - 2$

(L) $x^3 - 2x^2 + 5$

(S) $x^3 - x^2 - 2x - 4$

(R) $10x^2 - 9x - 25$

(L) $-3x^2 - 2x - 17$

(O) $-5x^3 - 5x - 4$

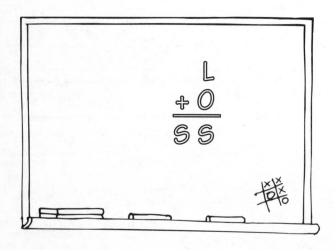

Answer: _____

© Good Apple GA16

me: _____ Date: _____ Class: _____

SPORTY HOST

The game of baseball was first played in the United States in 1829. Up until 1935, the games were always played in the daytime. Which city hosted the first nighttime baseball game?

Simplify each problem by using either the distributive property or the FOIL pattern. On the "scoreboard," mark a "run" for Cincinnati for every solution that ends in a negative number; mark a run for Dallas for every solution that ends in a positive number. The city with the most runs is the one that hosted the event.

 Tip: Use the left and right distributive properties when multiplying two polynomials. In other words, $(ax + b)(x^2 + x + c) = ax(x^2 + x + c) + b(x^2 + x + c)$ where a, b, and c are real numbers. Use the FOIL pattern when multiplying two binomials: $(x + b)(x + c) = x^2 + bx + cx + bc$, where b and c are real numbers.

1. $(x + 2)(x - 5)$

2. $(x - 4)(x^2 + 2x + 6)$

3. $(x + 3)(2x + 6)$

4. $(x + 2)(x^2 + 7x - 10)$

5. $(x^2 - 8)(x^2 + 3x - 1)$

6. $(3x^2 + 2)(x - 3)$

7. $(5x - 7)(3x - 4)$

8. $(x^2 + 4x - 2)(x + 4)$

9. $(-2x + 5)(x - 1)$

SCOREBOARD	
Cincinnati	**Dallas**

Answer: _____

Name: _____   Date: _____   Class: _____

ANIMAL TRACKS

Which animal can run faster than any other land animal, sprinting at speeds faster than 60 miles an hour?

Simplify each expression by multiplying the binomials. Shade in the grid boxes that contain your solutions. Read across the unshaded boxes to identify the answer to the puzzler.

 Tip: Use the two special patterns for multiplying binomials. They are the **sum and difference** pattern, where $(a + b)(a - b) = a^2 - b^2$, and the **square of the binomial** pattern, where $(a + b)^2 = a^2 + 2ab + b^2$ and $(a - b)^2 = a^2 - 2ab + b^2$. For example, $(2x - 3)^2 \rightarrow (2x)^2 - 2(2x)(3) + 3^2 \rightarrow 4x^2 - 12x + 9$.

1. $(x + 4)(x - 4)$

2. $(2x - 5)(2x + 5)$

3. $(5x + 1)^2$

4. $(3x - 2)^2$

5. $(2x - 6)(2x + 6)$

6. $(8x - 4)^2$

7. $(x + 6)(x - 6)$

8. $(x + 10)(x - 10)$

9. $(4x + 5)^2$

10. $(7x - 5)(7x + 5)$

11. $(6x - 4)^2$

12. $(3x + 9)^2$

13. $(9x + 4)(9x - 4)$

(C) $x^2 - 8x + 4$	(K) $x^2 - 36$	(A) $25x^2 + 10x + 1$	(H) $x^2 - 25$
(V) $16x^2 + 40x + 25$	(M) $9x^2 - 12x + 4$	(E) $x^2 + 6x + 9$	(D) $x^2 - 16$
(E) $x^2 - 121$	(N) $9x^2 + 54x + 81$	(L) $49x^2 - 25$	(B) $64x^2 - 64x + 16$
(U) $4x^2 - 25$	(C) $81x^2 - 16$	(T) $x^2 - 12x + 36$	(R) $x^2 - 100$
(Q) $36x^2 - 48x + 16$	(A) $100x^2 - 121$	(K) $4x^2 - 36$	(H) $x^2 - 14x + 49$

Answer: _____

Name: _____   Date: _____   Class: _____

HOW LOW CAN YOU GO?

This California area is the lowest place in North America. It is located
282 feet below sea level. What is the name of this area?

Factor each polynomial. As you solve each problem in numerical order, write on the "answer line"
the letter of the matching solution to spell out the two-word name of the geographic area.

 Tip: Factoring is the reverse of multiplying. There are two special patterns for factoring
polynomials: the **difference of two squares** pattern, where $a^2 - b^2 = (a + b)(a - b)$;
and the **perfect-square trinomial** pattern, where $a^2 + 2ab + b^2 = (a + b)^2$ and
$a^2 - 2ab + b^2 = (a - b)^2$. For example, $5x^2 - 20 \rightarrow 5(x^2 - 4) \rightarrow 5(x + 2)(x - 2)$.

1. $5x^2 - 125$

2. $x^2 + 6x + 9$

3. $x^2 - 64$

4. $x^2 - 4x + 4$

5. $9x^2 - 12x + 4$

6. $2x^3 - 32x$

7. $x^2 - 100$

8. $16x^2 + 40x + 25$

9. $49x^2 - 121$

10. $36x^2 - 48x + 16$

11. $4x^2 - 36$

(L) $(7x + 11)(7x - 11)$

(V) $2x(x + 4)(x - 4)$

(L) $(4x + 5)^2$

(A) $(x + 8)(x - 8)$

(A) $(x + 10)(x - 10)$

(Y) $4(x + 3)(x - 3)$

(T) $(x - 2)^2$

(H) $(3x - 2)^2$

(E) $(x + 3)^2$

(E) $(6x - 4)^2$

(D) $5(x + 5)(x - 5)$

Answer: _____

Name: _____   Date: _____   Class: _____

SCHOOL DAYS

It may look like a typical school sign, but there is a hidden meaning behind the cryptic message. Can you guess what it is?

Factor the polynomials and find the matching answers in the rows of school lockers. Write the corresponding letters on the numbered lines (labeled by exercise number) to spell out the two-word solution to the cryptic puzzler.

 Tip: When factoring polynomial $x^2 + bx + c$, identify factors of c whose sum is equal to b. If c is positive, the factors should have "like" signs; if c is negative, they should have "unlike" signs. For example, $x^2 + 3x - 10 = (x + 5)(x - 2)$. Always check your answers by multiplying the binomials to see if you get the original polynomial equation.

1. $x^2 - 6x - 16$

2. $x^2 - 5x + 6$

3. $x^2 + 10x + 21$

4. $2x^2 - x - 1$

5. $3x^2 + 5x + 2$

6. $x^2 - 12x + 32$

7. $3x^2 - 10x - 8$

8. $5x^2 - 7x - 6$

9. $x^2 + 16x + 63$

10. $5x^2 - x - 6$

SCHOOL

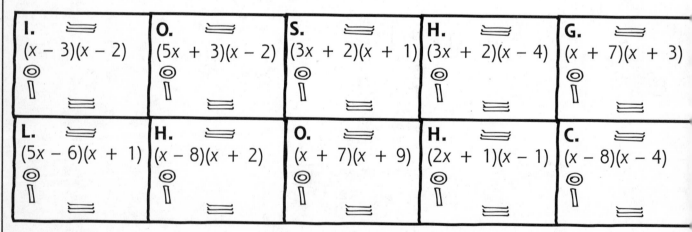

I. $(x - 3)(x - 2)$	O. $(5x + 3)(x - 2)$	S. $(3x + 2)(x + 1)$	H. $(3x + 2)(x - 4)$	G. $(x + 7)(x + 3)$
L. $(5x - 6)(x + 1)$	H. $(x - 8)(x + 2)$	O. $(x + 7)(x + 9)$	H. $(2x + 1)(x - 1)$	C. $(x - 8)(x - 4)$

Answer:

___ ___ ___ ___ ___ ___ ___ ___ ___ ___
1   2   3   4   5   6   7   8   9   10

Name: _____ Date: _____ Class: _____

MISS LIBERTY

If the Statue of Liberty were to walk off her pedestal and into a department store to do some shopping, at least how many feet high would the doorway have to be to allow her inside?

Draw a line connecting each quadratic equation in Column A to its matching solution in Column B. To spell out the answer to the "liberating" question, write in front of each exercise the letter representing its solution.

Tip: To solve a quadratic equation $ax^2 + bx + c = 0$, first factor the equation and then set each of the factors equal to zero and solve for the two values of x. For example, $x^2 + 7x + 12 = 0$ → $(x + 3)(x + 4) = 0$ → $(x + 3) = 0$ and $(x + 4) = 0$ → $x = -3$ and $x = -4$.

Column A

____ 1. $x^2 + 2x - 8 = 0$

____ 2. $x^2 + 10x + 25 = 0$

____ 3. $x^2 + 5x + 6 = 0$

____ 4. $x^2 - 11x + 30 = 0$

____ 5. $3x^2 + 5x + 2 = 0$

____ 6. $x^2 - 9x - 36 = 0$

____ 7. $5x^2 - x - 6 = 0$

____ 8. $x^2 + 6x - 7 = 0$

____ 9. $x^2 + 15x + 56 = 0$

____ 10. $4x^2 - x - 3 = 0$

____ 11. $x^2 - 7x - 18 = 2$

____ 12. $x^2 + 4x - 32 = 0$

____ 13. $5x^2 - 7x - 6 = 0$

____ 14. $6x^2 + 2x - 8 = 0$

____ 15. $8x^2 + 6x - 9 = 0$

Column B

(D) $x = -3/4, 1$

(E) $x = -2, -3$

(I) $x = -8, 4$

(R) $x = -7, 1$

(U) $x = -2/3, -1$

(O) $x = -4, 2$

(T) $x = -4/3, 1$

(N) $x = 1/2, -3$

(H) $x = 6, 5$

(F) $x = 9, -2$

(N) $x = -5$

(E) $x = -7, -8$

(F) $x = -3/5, 2$

(D) $x = 6/5, -1$

(Y) $x = -3/2, 3/4$

Answer: _____

Name: Date: Class:

REVIEW WHAT YOU KNOW
ABOUT SIMPLIFYING POLYNOMIALS

Add and subtract the following polynomials.

1. $(3x^2 + 2x + 4) + (5x^2 + 6x + 7)$

2. $(4x^2 + 7x + 2) - (9x^2 + 3x + 8)$

3. $(-8x^2 - 3x + 1) + (10x^2 - 7x - 3)$

4. $(-2x^2 - 5x + 6) - (11x^2 + 4x - 5)$

5. $(10x^3 + 15) + (2x^3 - 4x^2 - x + 3) - (13x^3 - 7x + 4)$

Use the FOIL pattern to multiply the following polynomials.

6. $(3x + 1)(5x - 7)$ 9. $(-3x - 6)(7x + 3)$

7. $(2x - 1)(3x + 4)$ 10. $(6x + 8)(-x - 9)$

8. $(4x + 5)(9x - 1)$

Use the distributive property to multiply the following polynomials.

11. $-4x^2 (5x^2 - 6x + 7)$ 14. $(2x + 7)(3x^2 - 8x - 11)$

12. $(2x + 1)(-3x - 10)$ 15. $(-5x^2 - 4x - 12)(8x - 2)$

13. $(x - 4)(6x + 9)$

Factor the following special products.

16. $16x^2 - 25$ 19. $49x^2 - 144$

17. $9x^2 + 12x + 4$ 20. $169x^2 - 81$

18. $x^2 - 10x + 25$

Factor the following trinomials.

21. $x^2 - 5x + 6$ 24. $6x^2 + 5x - 4$

22. $3x^2 + 11x + 10$ 25. $x^2 + 15x + 50$

23. $2x^2 - x - 21$

WORKING WITH REAL NUMBERS
River Rapids (p.9)
1. 5
2. 316
3. 9
4. 11
5. 1
6. 6
7. 8
8. 0
9. 44
10. 4
11. 15
12. 53
13. 12
14. 3
15. 10
16. 25
17. 24
18. 14

Answer: Africa

Good Owl Time (p.10)
A. 18
B. 96
C. 9
D. 16
E. 8
F. 19
G. 20
H. 131
I. 68
J. 73
K. 15
L. 121
M. 22
N. 170
O. 14
P. 42
R. 31
S. 38
T. 5
U. 49

Answer: At a hoo-tel.

Excuses (p.11)
1. −28
2. −4
3. 4
4. −20
5. −10
6. −19
7. −6
8. 5
9. 2
10. 3
11. −2
12. −5
13. 0
14. 8
15. −31
16. 2.9
17. −30.2
18. 1
19. −15.4
20. 3.5

Answer: I sat on my pencil and got lead poisoning!!

Gnarly Negatives (p.12)
1. 5
2. 7
3. −5
4. −11
5. −66
6. −18
7. −130
8. −15
9. −60
10. −2
11. −23
12. −4
13. −5.3
14. −8
15. 0

Answer: longest mustache

Rapid Rabbits (p.13)
A −4
B −27
C 24
E −3
H 113
I −150
K −47
L −118
M 12.5
O 8
P 9
Q −29
S 0
T −25
U −105
W 95
Y 5

Answer: Because they multiply so quickly without them.

Series of Multiplication (p.14)
1. −72a
2. −12a
3. −30a
4. −40a
5. −36a
6. 36a
7. −56a
8. −24a
9. −35a
10. 72a
11. 30a
12. 60a
13. −90a
14. 56a

Answer: New York Yankees

Chuggin' Through Multiplication (p.15)
N 30
F −60
O −120
M 64
U −36
R −182
A −72a
N −1408
T 105
D −576
A −240a
H −300
O 72a
A −336
L −720
F −160
M −24
U 0
I −54
L −3
E −200a
S −96

Answer: four and a half miles

Number Stumper (p.16)
1. True
2. True
3. False
4. True
5. False

Tree-mendous Math (p.17)
1. 6
2. 16
3. −5
4. −50
5. 3
6. 1/4
7. −1/4
8. 9
9. −1
10. 5
11. 28
12. −13

Answer: twigonometry

Review What You Know (p.18)
1. 15
2. 3
3. 29
4. 2
5. 39
6. 0
7. −5
8. −3
9. 11
10. −16
11. −48
12. −3y − 24
13. −1/3
14. 14x + 16
15. 1

SOLVING LINEAR EQUATIONS
Building Number Sense (p.19)

1	4	x		2	3	x
3	9	y		4	8	y
a	x		7	a	x	
	2	4	y			
	3	1	x		3	x
5	6	x		5	x	y
x	y			a	y	

Answer: 1,821 feet

Old Faithful (p.20)
1. 8x + 24y
2. 3r + 3s
3. 13x − 20y
4. x − 14y
5. 22x − 21
6. 15a − 5b
7. −3r − s
8. 17x − 13y
9. 36x
10. x + 2y
11. 5a + 14b
12. −11x − 19y
13. −26a − 47b
14. 0
15. −2a

Answer: Yellowstone

A Deeper Understanding (p.21)
1. P, x = −2
2. H, x = 45
3. I, x = −3
4. L, x = −5
5. I, x = −8
6. P, x = 4
7. P, x = −33
8. I, x = 11
9. N, x = 3
10. E, x = 1
11. S, x = −30

Answer: Philippines

Mid-Section Measurement (p.22)

	5	1			1	1		
	8	4			4	5		
2	3		3	7	4		1	4
8	7	6				6	9	6
8	8		8	7	5		6	0
	6	4			5	4		
	9	1			5	0		

Answer: 7,909 miles

Space Odyssey (p.23)
1. −15
2. 28
3. 10
4. −18
5. 26
6. 21
7. 12
8. −65
9. −24
10. 20
11. −72
12. −12
13. 24
14. 0
15. 32

Answer: Cape Canaveral

Singled Out (p.24)
1. A = 7; **B = 10**
2. E = 2; **I = 5**
3. **N = 4**; M = 3
4. H = 3; **G = 5**
5. **C = 12**; P = 6
6. **R = 9**; U = 2
7. I = 3; **O = 10**
8. T = 11; **S = 12**
9. **B = 8**; D = −20
10. V = −4; **Y = 0**

Answer: Bing Crosby

Supreme Justice (p.25)
1. −15
2. −1
3. −7
4. 3
5. 2
6. −2
7. 7
8. 1
9. −4
10. −3
11. 17
12. −5
13. 4
14. −6
15. 6
16. −8
17. 15
18. −12
19. 13
20. −11

Answer: Thurgood Marshall

Starry Sky (p.26)
1. 1
2. −5
3. −19
4. 2
5. −6
6. −1
7. −2

Answer: Polaris

Astonishing Astronaut (p.27)
1. $x = -y - 2$
2. $x = y - 6$
3. $x = y + 5$
4. $x = -3y + 10$
5. $x = -7y + 11$
6. $x = 3y + 8$
7. $x = 2y + 3$
8. $x = 3y - 4$
9. $x = 11y + 9$

Answer: gold stars

Review What You Know (p.28)
1. $6x$
2. $-9x$
3. $-3x$
4. $17x$
5. $-5x$
6. 5
7. −10
8. −13
9. −36
10. −2
11. 1
12. 1
13. 1
14. −1
15. 5
16. $x = -y + 9$
17. $x = -2y - 7$
18. $x = 2y - 4$
19. $x = -4y - 11$
20. $x = y - 4$

GRAPHING LINEAR EQUATIONS

Candy Craze (p.29)

1. 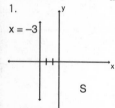 $x = -3$ S

5. 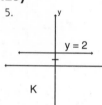 $y = 2$ K

2. 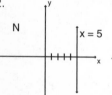 N $x = 5$

6. 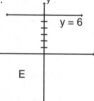 $y = 6$ E

3. 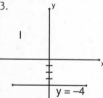 I $y = -4$

7. 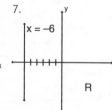 $x = -6$ R

4. 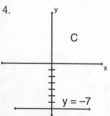 C $y = -7$

8. $x = 2$ S

Answer: Snickers

Crisscross (p.30)

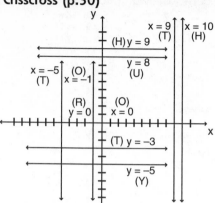

$x = 9$ (T) $x = 10$ (H)
(H) $y = 9$
$y = 8$ (U)
$x = -5$ (T) $x = -1$ (O)
(R) $y = 0$ (O) $x = 0$
(T) $y = -3$
$y = -5$ (Y)

Answer: Tooth Hurty

Colossal Creature (p.31)
1. (−2, 1) R
2. (6, −11) E
3. (−1, 1) D
4. (−2, 0) W
5. (1, 5) O
6. (−3, 2) O
7. (1, 0) D
8. (1, −3) T
9. (−2, 4) R
10. (−6, −7) E
11. (1/2, 6) E

Answer: redwood tree

Lights, Camera, Action! (p.32)

1. 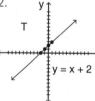 S $y = 3x + 4$

5. 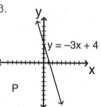 W $y = -2x - 1$

2. 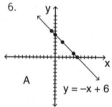 T $y = x + 2$

6. 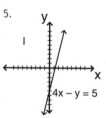 A $y = -x + 6$

3. 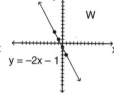 A $y = 2(x - 3)$

7. 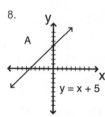 R $y = -(3x - 4)$

4. 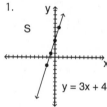 R $2x + 4y = 8$

8. 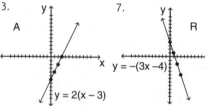 S $-x - 6y = 2$

Answer: Star Wars

Match Type (p.33)

1. 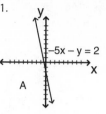 $-5x - y = 2$ A

6. 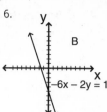 B $-6x - 2y = 1$

2. 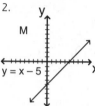 M $y = x - 5$

7. 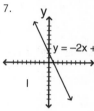 $y = -2x + 2$ I

3. 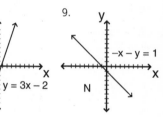 $y = -3x + 4$ P

8. A $y = x + 5$

4. H $y = 3x - 2$

9. $-x - y = 1$ N

5. I $4x - y = 5$

Answer: amphibian

Interception (p.34)
L. $x = -3$, $y = 9$
S. $x = -6$, $y = -3$
B. $x = -8$, $y = -12$
Y. $x = 9$, $y = 15$
C. $x = -12$, $y = 3$
D. $x = -4$, $y = -2$
L. $x = 7$, $y = 6$
O. $x = 5$, $y = -9$
A. $x = 3$, $y = -7$
W. $x = 5$, $y = -4$
S. $x = -26$, $y = -2$
O. $x = -3$, $y = -10$
A. $x = 3$, $y = -2$

Answer: Dallas Cowboys

ANSWER KEY

Graph–ic Design (p.35)

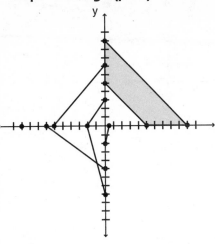

1. (–2, 0) (0, –8)
2. (–7, 0) (0, –5)
3. (1/2, 0) (0, –2)
4. (10, 0) (0, 10)
5. (–2, 0) (0, 3)
6. (5, 0) (0, 5)
7. (–6, 0) (0, 7)

Answer: A trapezoid is formed by equations four and six.

Winter Slopes (p.36)

1. –1/2
2. 0
3. 3
4. –3
5. 1
6. –1
7. 1/2
8. undefined
9. 2
10. 5
11. –2
12. 7

Answer: Alpine, Nordic

Young Master (p.37)

1. 0.3
2. 0
3. 0.05
4. 1.25
5. 0.32

Answer: Tiger

Amazing Animation (p.38)

1. 1/2, rises
2. –1, falls
3. undefined, vertical
4. 0, horizontal
5. 3, rises
6. –2, falls
7. 0, horizontal
8. undefined, vertical
9. –4, falls
10. 3, rises
11. 2, rises

Answer: The Simpsons

Wave of the Future (p.39)

1. line falls
2. line rises
3. horizontal line
4. line falls
5. vertical line
6. line falls
7. line rises
8. line rises

Answer: computer

Math Malady (p.40)

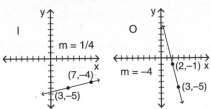

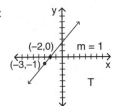

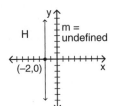

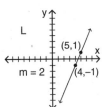

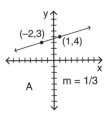

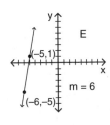

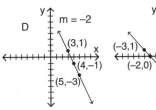

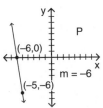

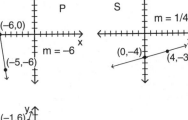

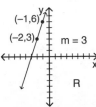

Answer: It had problems.

State Your Facts (p.41)

1. $y = 3/4x – 3$; $m = 3/4$; $b = –3$
2. $y = –2/5x – y$; $m = –2/5$; $b = –4$
3. $y = –x – 3$; $m = –1$; $b = –3$
4. $y = 5/6x – 5$; $m = 5/6$; $b = –5$
5. $y = 7/4x – 4$; $m = 7/4$; $b = –4$
6. $y = 8/3x + 4$; $m = 8/3$; $b = 4$
7. $y = 5x – 6$; $m = 5$; $b = –6$
8. $y = x – 2$; $m = 1$; $b = –2$
9. $y = 2/9x + 2$; $m = 2/9$; $b = 2$
10. $y = x/3 + 7$; $m = 1/3$; $b = 7$
11. $y = 6x + 10$; $m = 6$; $b = 10$
12. $y = x + 13$; $m = 1$; $b = 13$

Answer: Ohio

Intriguing Invention (p.42)

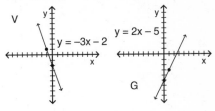

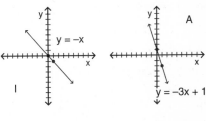

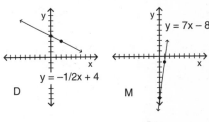

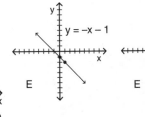

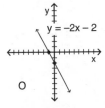

Answer: video game

ANSWER KEY

Astonishing Apple (p.43)

1. $y = 2x$

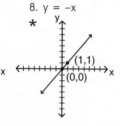
(1,2) (0,0) *

2. $y = -x - 4$

(3,1) (0,-1)

3. $y = x + 3$

(-1,-3) (0,-4)

4. $y = -7x + 2$

(-1,1) (0,0)

5. $y = -1/6x + 6$

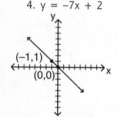
(0,3) (1,4)

6. $y = 5x - 5$

(-1,-4) (0,-7)

7. $y = 2/3x - 1$

(0,2) (1,-5)

8. $y = -x$
*

(1,1) (0,0)

9. $y = -3x - 7$

(0,6) (6,5)

10. $y = x$
*

(0,5) (4,2)

11. $y = -3/4x + 5$

(1,0) (0,-5)

12. $y = 6x - 2$

(1,4) (0,-2)

Answer: three

＊Note: Marks the graphs that pass through only 2 points.

Review What You Know (p.44)

1.

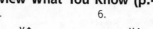

2.

3.

4.

5.

6.

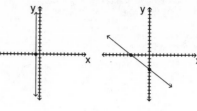

7.

8.

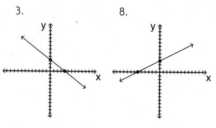

9.

10.

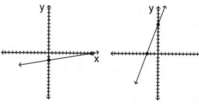

11. −1, falls
12. undefined, vertical
13. 5, rises
14. 0, horizontal
15. 2, rises

16. $y = 1/2x - 2$
    $b = -2$
    $m = 1/2$

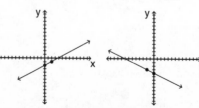

17. $y = -1/2x - 4$
    $b = -4$
    $m = -1/2$

18. $y = x - 7$
    $b = 7$
    $m = 1$

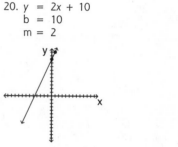

19. $y = -7x - 9$
    $b = -9$
    $m = -7$

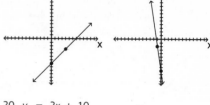

20. $y = 2x + 10$
    $b = 10$
    $m = 2$

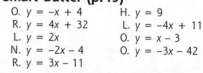

WRITING LINEAR EQUATIONS

Positive Thinking (p.45)

1. $y = 2x - 5$	8. $y = -10x - 9$
2. $y = 1/3x + 2$	9. $y = 8x - 1/2$
3. $y = -4x - 3$	10. $y = 2x + 1/3$
4. $y = -1/2x + 8$	11. $y = -x$
5. $y = -3x - 4$	12. $y = x - 1$
6. $y = -1/3x - 2$	13. $y = -5$
7. $y = -5x + 2$	14. $y = -x - 1$

Answer: Clear your mind of can't.

Fast Track (p.46)

I. $y = 2x - 10$	P. $y = 6x + 5$
N. $y = x - 6$	M. $y = -x + 10$
U. $y = 5x + 3$	C. $y = -1/2x - 3$
T. $y = -7x + 26$	P. $y = 9x + 32$
E. $y = 4x + 38$	

Answer: Pentium PC

Planet Intellect (p.47)

O. $y = 3/4x - 3$	M. $y = 5x - 6$
E. $y = -2/5x - 4$	B. $y = x - 2$
O. $y = -x - 3$	T. $y = 2/9x + 2$
S. $y = 5/6x - 5$	K. $y = 1/3x + 7$
C. $y = 7/4x - 4$	O. $y = 6x + 10$

Answer: comet books

Greek Games (p.48)

1. $y = 2x - 8$	5. $y = -3x + 17$
2. $y = -2x + 4$	6. $y = -2x$
3. $y = -3x + 28$	7. $y = 3x + 2$
4. $y = 2x + 1$	8. $y = 3x + 9$

Answer: footrace

Smart Butter (p.49)

O. $y = -x + 4$	H. $y = 9$
R. $y = 4x + 32$	L. $y = -4x + 11$
L. $y = 2x$	O. $y = x - 3$
N. $y = -2x - 4$	O. $y = -3x - 42$
R. $y = 3x - 11$	

Answer: honor roll

ANSWER KEY

Sizing Up Sand (p.50)

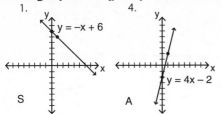

1. S
2. A
3. H
4. A
5. R
6. A

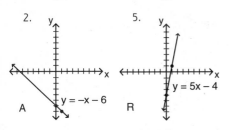
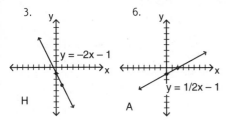

Answer: Sahara

Let's Get to the Point (p.51)

1. $3x + y = 3$
2. $x + y = -6$
3. $-x + 7y = 28$
4. $-5x + y = -8$
5. $4x + y = 6$
6. $-7x + y = 9$
7. $-3x - 4y = 2$
8. $5x + 6y = -4$
9. $-x - 10y = 20$
10. $2x - 7y = -7$
11. $8x - 4y = 20$
12. $-9x - 9y = 26$
13. $7x + 6y = -1$
14. $-5x + 2y = 16$
15. $-12x + 11y = 17$
16. $3x - 2y = 14$

Answer: graphite

Let the Music Play (p.52)

1. $10x + y = 4$
2. $-3x + y = 7$
3. $-2x + y = 1$
4. $7x + y = -9$
5. $-8x + y = -7$
6. $6x + y = -16$
7. $2x + y = -3$
8. $x + y = 4$
9. $-8x + y = -5$
10. $x + y = 12$
11. $-x + y = -3$

Answer: Paul McCartney

Elderly Animal (p.53)

1. $y - 5 = 4(x + 4)$
2. $y - 8 = -2(x - 7)$
3. $y + 4 = 2(x + 1)$
4. $y - 9 = 7(x - 3)$
5. $y - 6 = 3(x + 4)$
6. $y + 8 = -2(x + 7)$
7. $y - 9 = -7(x + 3)$
8. $y - 3 = -3(x + 8)$
9. $y + 6 = 6(x + 2)$
10. $y + 9 = 5(x + 7)$
11. $y + 3 = -2(x + 3)$
12. $y + 9 = 8(x + 10)$
13. $y - 9 = -8(x - 10)$
14. $y - 3 = 3(x + 3)$
15. $y - 6 = -6(x - 2)$

Answer: giant tortoise

Review What You Know (p.54)

1. $y = 3x - 4$
2. $y = -x + 5$
3. $y = -6x - 7$
4. $y = 8x + 12$
5. $y = -2x - 9$
6. $y = 2x - 12$
7. $y = x + 3$
8. $y = 3x - 7$
9. $y = -2x - 12$
10. $y = -3x - 2$
11. $2x + y = 5$
12. $-3x + y = -7$
13. $5x + y = -9$
14. $4x - y = 10$
15. $x + 2y = 6$
16. $y - 4 = -8(x + 3)$
17. $y - 2 = 10(x + 1)$
18. $y + 6 = -3(x - 5)$
19. $y + 2 = 7(x + 8)$
20. $y + 10 = -6(x - 9)$

CALCULATING ABSOLUTE VALUES & INEQUALITIES

Creative Combinations (p.55)

1. $y = -2, -8, -4, -6, -10$;
   answer: Libra
2. $y = -2, -1, -10, 0, 3, -6$;
   answer: loafer
3. $y = -19, -10, -8, 1, 3, -6$;
   answer: waiter

Richie Rich (p.56)

1. $x = -3, 7$
2. $x = 3, -17$
3. $x = 5, 3$
4. $x = 4, -2$
5. $x = 19, -13$
6. $x = -2, 14$
7. $x = 15, -19$
8. $x = 0, 10$
9. $x = 20, -22$
10. $x = 2, -6$
11. $x = 8, -2$
12. $x = -6/5, 2$

Answer: Walton family

Animal Mix-Up (p.57)

1. $(2, 6)$
2. $(-3, -4)$
3. $(-5, -7)$
4. $(1, 0)$
5. $(-9, -9)$
6. $(8, 0)$
7. $(0, -2)$
8. $(-4, -5)$
9. $(5, 0)$
10. $(0, 0)$
11. $(-6, -6)$
12. $(0, -8)$
13. $(-1, -1)$
14. $(-7, -7)$
15. $(-8, 0)$

Answer: scale

Sizable City (p.58)

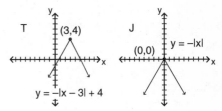
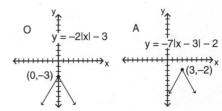
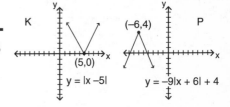
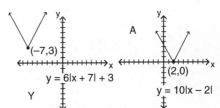
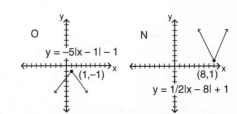

Answer: Tokyo, Japan

ANSWER KEY

Absolute Winners (p.59)

1.
$y = -3|x - 2| + 4$
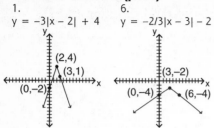
(2,4)
(3,1)
(0,−2)

6.
$y = -2/3|x - 3| - 2$
(3,−2)
(0,−4) (6,−4)

2.
$y = |x + 3| - 5$
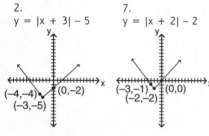
(−4,−4) (0,−2)
(−3,−5)

7.
$y = |x + 2| - 2$
(−3,−1) (0,0)
(−2,−2)

3.
$y = 5|x + 4| - 6$
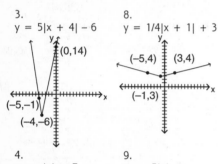
(0,14)
(−5,−1)
(−4,−6)

8.
$y = 1/4|x + 1| + 3$
(−5,4) (3,4)
(−1,3)

4.
$y = -|x| + 7$

(0,7)
(−3,4) (3,4)

9.
$y = -5|x|$
(0,0)
(−1,−5) (1,−5)

5.
$y = 2|x - 1|$
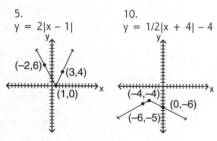
(−2,6)
(3,4)
(1,0)

10.
$y = 1/2|x + 4| - 4$
(−4,−4) (0,−6)
(−6,−5)

Answer: five

Public Record (p.60)

1. $x > -9$
2. $x > -6$
3. $x \le -3$
4. $x \ge 2$
5. $x < 6$
6. $x \le 12$
7. $x < 77$
8. $x < -9$
9. $x \le 11$
10. $x < -90$
11. $x \ge 98$
12. $x > 2$
13. $x \le -92$
14. $x < 32$
15. $x \ge -33$
16. $x > 12$

Answer: Santa Fe, New Mexico

Kiss Undercover (p.61)

1. $x < 5$
2. $x \le 1$
3. $x < 10$
4. $x > -7$
5. $x \ge 6$
6. $x < 11$
7. $x < -4$
8. $x \ge 12$
9. $x > 8$
10. $x < 6$
11. $x < 7$
12. $x \ge 9$
13. $x < -1$
14. $x \ge 2$
15. $x > 20$
16. $x \ge -5$

Answer: five square inches

On the Right Track (p.62)

1. $1 < x < 1\ 1/2$
2. $-2 > x > -3$
3. $2 \ge x \ge 1$
4. $-4 < x < -1$
5. $3/2 < x < 9/2$
6. $1 \le x \le 3$
7. $1 > x \ge -3$
8. $2 \le x < 5$
9. $7 > x > 6$
10. $4 < x < 6$
11. $1 < x \le 4$
12. $1 < x < 3$

Answer: six

Tasty Geography (p.63)

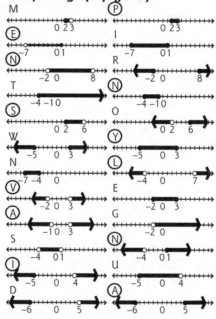

Answer: Pennsylvania

Tall Talent (p.64)

1. $x < -1$ or $x > 5$
2. $-6 \le x \le 4$
3. $2 < x < 6$
4. $x \le -1$ or $x \ge 3$
5. $x > -3$ or $x < -13$
6. $2 < x < 3$
7. $x \ge -2$ or $x \le -4$
8. $2 < x < 18$
9. $x > 2$ or $x < -18/5$
10. $x \le 5/3$ or $x \ge 3$
11. $-14 < x < 6$

Answer: Michael J. Fox

Money Math (p.65)

1. no
2. yes
3. yes
4. yes
5. yes
6. no
7. no
8. yes
9. yes
10. no
11. yes
12. no
13. yes
14. yes
15. yes
16. no

Answer: ten dollar bill

Matching Measures (p.66)

1. E
2. E
3. M
4. R
5. T

Answer: meter

Record Race (p.67)

1. $5x - 5y \le 10$
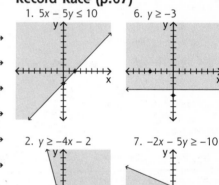

6. $y \ge -3$

2. $y \ge -4x - 2$
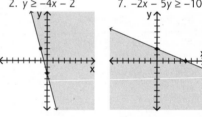

7. $-2x - 5y \ge -10$

3. $x - 2y \ge -4$
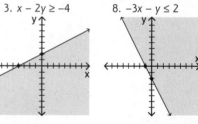

8. $-3x - y \le 2$

4. $y \ge -4$
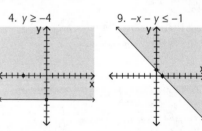

9. $-x - y \le -1$

5. $6x - 8y \ge -24$
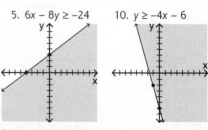

10. $y \ge -4x - 6$

Answer: seven

Review What You Know (p.68)

1. $x = 12, -2$
2. $x = 13, -19$
3. $x = 9/4, -15/4$
4. $x = 1, 8$
5. $x = -8, -2$
6.

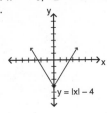

$y = |x| - 4$

7.

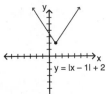

$y = |x - 1| + 2$

8.

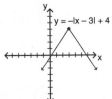

$y = -|x - 3| + 4$

9.

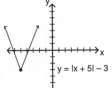

$y = |x + 5| - 3$

10.

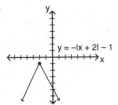

$y = -|x + 2| - 1$

11. $x < 3$

12. $x \leq 9$

13. $-2 \leq x \leq 8$

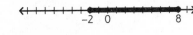

14. $x \leq -7$ or $x \geq 1$

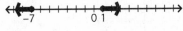

15. $-1 < x < 8$

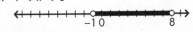

16. $x \leq -2$

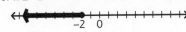

17. $1 < x < 7$

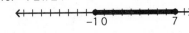

18. $-1 \leq x \leq 7$

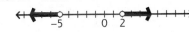

19. $x > 2$ or $x < -5$

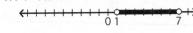

20. $-4 \leq x \leq -2$

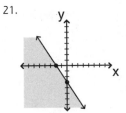

21.

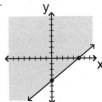

22.

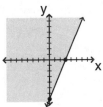

23.

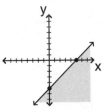

24.

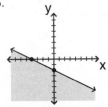

25.

SOLVING LINEAR SYSTEMS

Quadrilateral Question (p.69)

1. (3, 1/2)
2. (-2, 5)
3. (4, 1)
4. (5, -1)
5. (-1, 2)
6. (3/4, 1)
7. (-2, 10)
8. (-1, -1)
9. (1/4, -3)
10. (2, 2)

Answer: trapezoids

Record Breaker (p.70)

1. (0, -5)

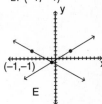

P   (0,-5)

2. (-1, -1)

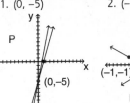

(-1,-1)   E

3. (5, -2)

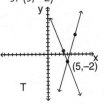

(5,-2)   T

4. (1, 1)

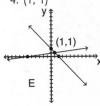

(1,1)   E

5. (1, 1)

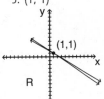

(1,1)   R

6. (2, 0)

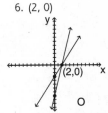

(2,0)   O

7. (1, 3)

(1,3)   S

8. (3, 3)

(3,3)   E

Answer: Pete Rose

Hammin' It Up (p.71)

M. (1, 3)
F. (4, 3)
A. (-2, -4)
S. (-1, 2)
C. (5, 3)
H. (-1, 1)
U. (0, 0)
F. (2, 4)

Answer: hamcuffs

Monstrous Mammal (p.72)
1. (−7, 3)
2. (1/2, 2)
3. (5, 10)
4. (−2, 3)
5. (−10, −25)
6. (−7, 10)
7. (3, 14)
8. (−1, 8)
9. (2, −2)

Answer: blue whale

Mythical Math (p.73)
1. (4, −2)
2. (−1, 3)
3. (−2, −2)
4. (8, 1)
5. (2, 3)
6. (1, 1)
7. (6, 5)
8. (−4, 1)

Answer: Pegasus

Batter Up (p.74)
1. many
2. none
3. many
4. none
5. many
6. none
7. none
8. none
9. none

Answer: home plate

Tasty Treat (p.75)
1. Quadrants I, III, and IV
2. Quadrants I and IV
3. Quadrant IV
4. Quadrants I, II, and III
5. Quadrants I, II, III, and IV
6. Quadrants II and III
7. Quadrant I
8. Quadrant III

Answer: lollipop

Review What You Know (p.76)
1. (−1, 2)
2. (1/2, 3)
3. (2, 0)
4. (3, 4)
5. (1, 2)
6. (3, 1)
7. (7, 4)
8. (1, −1)
9. (2, 1)
10. (3, −4)

11. no solution

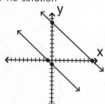

12. same line, many solutions

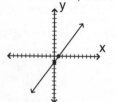

13.

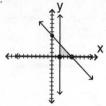

14.

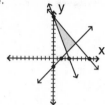

WORKING WITH EXPONENTS
Believe It or Not (p.77)
1. 3^6
2. x^{15}
3. $-64x^6$
4. x^8
5. 144
6. $56x^{15}$
7. $36x^2$
8. $81x^5$
9. $(7 + x)^{12}$
10. $-8x^{10}$

Answer: motorcycle

Shaping Up (p.78)
1. x^{15}
2. $4x^2$
3. $64x^9$
4. x^4y^6
5. $64x^{12}$
6. $-24x^2y^2$
7. $9x^3$
8. $8x^4y^4$
9. x^5y^4
10. $-64x^6$
11. $-16x^9$
12. $25x^4y^4$
13. $8x^{12}$
14. $-72x^5y^6$
15. $25x^5$
16. $27x^7y^4z^7$
17. $-81x^{10}$
18. $-27x^{12}y^4z^{19}$

Answers: pentagon, rhombus, parallelogram

Presidential State (p.79)
1. 16
2. −4
3. −8
4. 32
5. 8
6. 64
7. 128
8. 256
9. 81
10. 52

Answer: Washington

Ancient Calculator (p.80)
1. $1/x^5$
2. y^4/x^3
3. y^3/x^6
4. x^2y^3
5. y/x
6. $1/y^3$
7. 1
8. $3/(4xy^2)$
9. y^2
10. $1/(25x^2)$
11. $3x^4/y^3$
12. $-4/y^5$

Answer: abacus

In the Blink of an Eye (p.81)
1. 5
2. 8/27
3. 1/16
4. 6/5
5. 1/9
6. 32
7. −125
8. 25
9. 1
10. −1
11. 16
12. 343
13. 27
14. 49/16
15. 1/64
16. 9

Answer: fifteen times

Plastic Problems (p.82)

	2	3		2	9	
2		1	1	0		1
4	1		7		1	6
	1	9		3	0	
2	8		4		5	1
6		1	0	3		8
	3	4		2	7	

Answer: 400 years

Exponent Assignment (p.83)
M. 36
U. 1
O. −9
K. 1/16
T. −25
H. −1/2
R. −1
C. 9
O. 1/100
W. −3
H. 7
W. −3
E. 5
M. 4
O. 121

Answer: Two much homework!

Whiggish Republican (p.84)
1. 134,560
2. 4,500
3. 0.07803
4. 0.0000839
5. 52,300,000
6. 0.00013
7. 0.751
8. 7.51×10^{-4}
9. 7.51×10^{-3}
10. 7.51×10^{4}
11. 7.51×10^{8}
12. 7.51×10^{3}
13. 7.51×10^{-7}
14. 7.51×10

Answer: Abraham Lincoln

Award-Winning Math (p.85)
1. 3.6×10^{7}
2. 1.55×10^{7}
3. 1.59×10
4. 2.1×10^{3}
5. 4.48×10^{7}
6. 2.28×10^{5}
7. 1.77×10^{2}
8. 3.43×10^{-1}
9. 3.59×10^{-1}
10. 2.18×10^{2}
11. 1.47×10^{-6}

Answer: Forrest Gump

Review What You Know (p.86)
1. 1/9
2. 25
3. 1
4. 1
5. 1/16
6. 5
7. $-8x^5$
8. $-1/16a$
9. $2x^2y^3$
10. 10/y
11. 0.00254
12. 31,000
13. 0.0725
14. 92,600,000
15. 0.000000043
16. 9.6×10^{-7}
17. 1.23×10^{8}
18. 4.1×10^{-4}
19. 8.4×10^{6}
20. 8.7×10^{-6}

SOLVING SQUARE ROOTS AND QUADRATIC EQUATIONS

Declaring Independence (p.87)
1. 8
2. −7
3. 0
4. −1
5. undefined
6. 9
7. −12
8. 0.4
9. 25
10. −16
11. 7.21

12. −10
13. −11
14. 6
15. 3/2
16. −7/6
17. 5/13
18. −1/8
19. −3.32
20. 0.5

Answer: New Hampshire

Moon Walk (p.88)
1. ± 4
2. ± 7
3. ± 10
4. ± 5
5. 0
6. ± 8
7. ± 15
8. no solution
9. ± 3
10. ± 1
11. ± 1/3
12. ± 6
13. ± 1/2

Answer: Neil Armstrong

Tool' through Math (p.89)
1. 7.21
2. 11.40
3. 8.54
4. 14.28
5. 27.57
6. 36.77
7. 35.21
8. 6.32
9. 10.39
10. 17.35
11. 26.46

Answer: multipliers

Quazy Quadratic (p.90)
1. $x = -6, -9$
2. $x = 2, -4$
3. $x = -5, -2$
4. $x = 4, -5$
5. $x = 7, 1/3$
6. $x = 8/3, -2$
7. $x = -4/5, 2$
8. $x = 5/7, -2$
9. $x = -1, -2$
10. $x = 1/2, 2$

Answer: Not up to par

Home Run (p.91)
1. 16, two solutions
2. −32, none
3. 0, one solution
4. −47, none
5. 44, two solutions
6. −4, none
7. 0, one solution
8. 21, two solutions
9. 1, two solutions
10. 0, one solution

Answer: three

Perplexing Parabolas (p.92)
1. (1, 9), opens down
2. (−2, −23), opens up
3. (1/2, 21/4), opens down
4. (0, 0), opens up
5. (0, −10), opens down
6. (−1, −5), opens down
7. (2, 4), opens down
8. (−4, −17), opens up
9. (−2, 19), opens down
10. (−4, 4), opens up

Answer: four

Many Multiples (p.93)

1. $y = 2x^2 + 8x - 4$
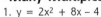

6. $y = -x^2 + 2x - 1$

2. $y = x^2 + 4x + 3$
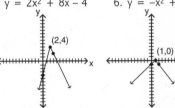

7. $y = x^2 + 5$

3. $y = -x^2$
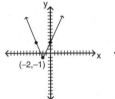

8. $y = 4x^2 + 16x + 20$
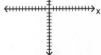

4. $y = -x^2 - 6$
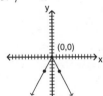

9. $y = -5x^2 - 20x - 19$
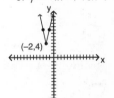

5. $y = -3x^5 - 18x - 25$
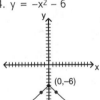

10. $y = x^2 + 6x + 4$
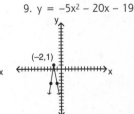

Answer: four

ANSWER KEY

Review What You Know (p.94)

1. ± 4
2. ± 5
3. ± 1/2
4. ± 4
5. ± 11
6. $c = 5$
7. $b = 8$
8. $a = 7.48$
9. $c = 15$
10. $a = 21$
11. $x = 2, -4/5$
12. $x = -2, -1$
13. $x = 1/3, 7$
14. $x = 4, -5$
15. $x = 1/2, 2$
16.

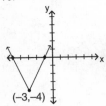

(−3,−4)

17.

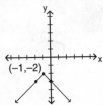

(−1,−2)

SIMPLIFYING POLYNOMIALS

Secret Shape (p.95)

1. $4x^2 + 4x + 9$
2. $8x^2 + 6x + 2$
3. $10x^2 - x + 8$
4. $-5x^2 - 1$
5. $-5x^2 + 3x + 4$
6. $-12x^2 - 5x + 7$
7. $9x^2 - 10x + 2$
8. $x^3 + x^2$
9. $3x^3 + 3x^2 + 6$
10. $-3x^2 - x - 8$
11. $-2x^2 - 4x + 6$
12. $13x^3 - 9x^2 - 6x$
13. $4x^2 + 2x + 1$
14. $x^3 - x^2 + 14$
15. $-8x^2 + 3x - 2$
16. $5x^3 - 2x^2 - 5$

Answers: chord, sector, radius, circumference; circle

Puzzling Problem (p.96)

1. $x + 1$
2. $-x^2 + 11x + 1$
3. $-11x^3 - 2x^2 + 7x$
4. $2x^2 + 3x + 2$
5. $-3x^2 - 2x - 17$
6. $x^3 - 2x^2 + 5$
7. $-5x^3 - 5x - 4$
8. $-3x^2 - 6x + 4$
9. $x^3 - x^2 - 2x - 4$

Answer: total loss

Sporty Host (p.97)

1. $x^2 - 3x - 10$
2. $x^3 - 2x^2 - 2x - 24$
3. $2x^2 + 12x + 18$
4. $x^3 + 9x^2 + 4x - 20$
5. $x^4 + 3x^3 - 9x^2 - 24x + 8$
6. $3x^3 - 9x^2 + 2x - 6$
7. $15x^2 - 41x + 28$
8. $x^3 + 8x^2 + 14x - 8$
9. $-2x^2 + 7x - 5$

Answer: Cincinnati

Animal Tracks (p.98)

1. $x^2 - 16$
2. $4x^2 - 25$
3. $25x^2 + 10x + 1$
4. $9x^2 - 12x + 4$
5. $4x^2 - 36$
6. $64x^2 - 64x + 16$
7. $x^2 - 36$
8. $x^2 - 100$
9. $16x^2 + 40x + 25$
10. $49x^2 - 25$
11. $36x^2 - 48x + 16$
12. $9x^2 + 54x + 81$
13. $81x^2 - 16$

Answer: cheetah

How Low Can You Go? (p.99)

1. $5(x + 5)(x - 5)$
2. $(x + 3)^2$
3. $(x + 8)(x - 8)$
4. $(x - 2)^2$
5. $(3x - 2)^2$
6. $2x(x + 4)(x - 4)$
7. $(x + 10)(x - 10)$
8. $(4x + 5)^2$
9. $(7x + 11)(7x - 11)$
10. $(6x - 4)^2$
11. $4(x + 3)(x - 3)$

Answer: Death Valley

School Days (p.100)

1. $(x - 8)(x + 2)$
2. $(x - 3)(x - 2)$
3. $(x + 7)(x + 3)$
4. $(2x + 1)(x - 1)$
5. $(3x + 2)(x + 1)$
6. $(x - 8)(x - 4)$
7. $(3x + 2)(x - 4)$
8. $(5x + 3)(x - 2)$
9. $(x + 7)(x + 9)$
10. $(5x - 6)(x + 1)$

Answer: high school

Miss Liberty (p.101)

1. $x = -4, 2$
2. $x = -5$
3. $x = -2, -3$
4. $x = 6, 5$
5. $x = -2/3, -1$
6. $x = 12, -3$
7. $x = 6/5, -1$
8. $x = -7, 1$
9. $x = -7, -8$
10. $x = -3/4, 1$
11. $x = 9, -2$
12. $x = -8, 4$
13. $x = -3/5, 2$
14. $x = -4/3, 1$
15. $x = -3/2, 3/4$

Answer: One hundred fifty

Review What You Know (p.102)

1. $8x^2 + 8x + 11$
2. $-5x^2 + 4x - 6$
3. $2x^2 - 10x - 2$
4. $-13x^2 - 9x + 11$
5. $-x^3 - 4x^2 + 6x + 14$
6. $15x^2 - 16x - 7$
7. $6x^2 + 5x - 4$
8. $36x^2 + 41x - 5$
9. $-21x^2 - 51x - 18$
10. $-6x^2 - 62x - 72$
11. $-20x^4 + 24x^3 - 28x^2$
12. $-6x^2 - 23x - 10$
13. $6x^2 - 15x - 36$
14. $6x^3 + 5x^2 - 78x - 56$
15. $-40x^3 - 22x^2 - 88x + 24$
16. $(4x + 4)(4x - 5)$
17. $(3x + 2)^2$
18. $(x - 5)^2$
19. $(7x + 12)(7x - 12)$
20. $(13x + 9)(13x - 9)$
21. $(x - 2)(x - 3)$
22. $(3x + 5)(x + 2)$
23. $(2x - 7)(x + 3)$
24. $(2x - 1)(3x + 4)$
25. $(x + 5)(x + 10)$